WHISPERS OF INNER STRENGTH

WHISPERS OF INNER STRENGTH

RAYAN MUSK

Spectra Enterprise

CONTENTS

INDEX

Introduction

In the many-sided embroidery of human life, a fragile exchange of feelings, encounters, and versatility unfurls. Life, with its horde challenges, frequently murmurs to us in the unobtrusive language of inward strength. It is in these murmurs that the significant quintessence of human perseverance, steadiness, and mental fortitude falsehoods, ready to be uncovered. The excursion of self-revelation, the journey for reason, and the tireless quest for development are completely entwined in the texture of internal strength.

At the center of this account is the acknowledgment that strength isn't generally clearly and self-assured; it frequently uncovers itself in the peaceful minutes, the quieted discussions inside the offices of the spirit. Murmurs of internal strength reverberation through the hallways of our psyches, encouraging us to stand up to difficulty, embrace weakness, and rise above our impediments. It is in these murmurs that the seeds of flexibility are planted, flourishing in the ripe soil of the human soul.

To comprehend the meaning of these murmurs, one should dive into the intricacy of the human mind and the elements of self-awareness. The idea of inward strength rises above the actual domain, venturing into the domains of close to home, mental, and otherworldly determination. A power pushes people forward, directing them through the maze of life's difficulties and vulnerabilities.

The murmurs of internal strength frequently manifest in snapshots of isolation, where the racket of the outside world disappears, leaving space for reflection and self-disclosure. In the quietude of self-reflection, people might hear the weak reverberations of their internal strength, an unobtrusive update that they have the flexibility to explore the blustery oceans of life. This inside exchange turns into a compass, directing them through the violent waters and assisting them with tracking down their direction back to the shores of steadiness.

Also, the murmurs of internal strength are not held for snapshots of emergency alone. They go with people in their ordinary interests, pushing them to continue on despite difficulties, embrace vulnerability, and develop a mentality of development. It is a continuous discussion with oneself, a steady certification that flexibility isn't an objective yet an excursion — one that unfurls with each step taken and each challenge survive.

The beginning of inward strength frequently lies in the pot of affliction. When confronted with life's preliminaries, people have the chance to take advantage of repositories of solidarity they might not have known existed. It is in these difficult minutes that the murmurs of internal strength become more articulated, offering comfort, direction, and a feeling of direction. Misfortune, as opposed to being a power that lessens, turns into a pot that refines, forming people into more grounded, stronger variants of themselves.

Firmly interweaved with inward strength is the idea of weakness. The capacity to embrace one's weaknesses is a demonstration of genuine strength, as it requires a profound comprehension of oneself and a readiness to defy the inborn delicacy of the human experience. The murmurs of inward strength urge people to recognize their weaknesses not as shortcomings but rather as pathways to development and self-disclosure.

Besides, the murmurs of internal strength resound in the tales of people who have conquered apparently outlandish chances. These accounts act as guides of motivation, enlightening the groundbreaking force of flexibility and the relentless soul that lives inside every individual. Whether in the pages of history, the stories of regular legends, or the narratives of individual victories, the murmurs of internal strength reverberation across existence, winding around an aggregate embroidery of human flexibility.

The investigation of internal strength stretches out past the singular domain and envelops the elements of relational connections and local area flexibility. In the interconnected snare of human associations, the murmurs of internal strength become a common story, restricting people together in snapshots of aggregate test and win. Networks that develop a culture of internal strength are better prepared to explore difficulties, support each other, and cultivate a feeling of solidarity in variety.

Besides, the murmurs of inward strength assume a crucial part in forming cultural stories and impacting social ideal models. The versatility of a general public is much of the time reflected in its aggregate capacity to draw strength from the inside, cultivating a culture that values steadiness, sympathy, and shared liability. As social orders wrestle with complex issues going from worldwide pandemics to financial incongruities, the murmurs of internal strength become a binding together power, moving aggregate activity and flexibility.

In the domain of emotional well-being, the murmurs of inward strength hold significant importance. The excursion to mental prosperity frequently includes the development of inward versatility, the capacity to explore the recurring patterns of feelings, and the fortitude to look for help when required. In reality as we know it where the shame encompassing emotional wellness perseveres, the murmurs of inward strength advocate for sympathy, understanding, and the acknowledgment that looking for help is definitely not an indication of shortcoming however a brave step towards mending.

Otherworldliness, as well, is complicatedly connected with the murmurs of internal strength. Across different otherworldly practices, the idea of internal strength is integral to the way of self-acknowledgment and illumination. The murmurs guide searchers on an excursion of reflection, self-control, and association with a higher reason, cultivating a significant feeling of internal harmony and peacefulness.

In the instructive scene, the development of internal strength is an essential component in sustaining strong, versatile, and enabled people. The murmurs of inward strength empower a development outlook, imparting in students the conviction that difficulties are potential open doors for learning and self-improvement. Teachers, as facilitators of development, assume a vital part in enhancing these murmurs, establishing a climate that engages understudies to defeat deterrents and open their maximum capacity.

In the corporate world, the murmurs of inward strength become a directing power for pioneers and workers the same. Associations that focus on the prosperity and versatility of their labor force make a culture of strengthening and development. Pioneers who stand by listening to the murmurs of internal strength inside themselves and their groups encourage a climate where difficulties are met with a cooperative soul, and mishaps become venturing stones to progress.

As we explore the intricacies of the cutting edge world, the murmurs of internal strength coax us to search internally, to take advantage of the wellspring of versatility that lives inside every one of us. They advise us that strength is certainly not a scant asset however a bountiful power that can be developed and shared. In a world that frequently stresses outside proportions of progress, the murmurs of internal strength call us to rethink how we might interpret strength, to embrace weakness, and to perceive that genuine power lies in the legitimacy of our human experience.

All in all, Murmurs of Inward Strength is an ensemble of versatility, a story that unfurls in the tranquil snapshots of self-reflection, the pots of misfortune, and the aggregate soul of networks. An immortal tune reverberates across the embroidery of human experience, directing people on an excursion of self-disclosure, development, and strengthening. As we stand by listening to these murmurs, we open the groundbreaking force of inward strength, embracing the completion of our humankind and outlining a course towards a stronger, merciful, and associated world.

Chapter 1

Awakening the Whisper Within

In the peaceful openings of our psyches, there exists a murmur — an unobtrusive mumble that frequently slips through the cracks in the midst of the bedlam of regular daily existence. This murmur is the voice of our internal identities, a repository of undiscovered possibility and intelligence ready to be stirred. In the excursion of self-revelation, we frequently end up exploring through the maze of outside impacts, cultural assumptions, and the persevering quest for progress. In any case, in the midst of the bedlam, there lies a significant truth: the way to opening our fullest possible exists in.

Arousing the murmur inside is certainly not a simple endeavor; a significant excursion requires mental fortitude, thoughtfulness, and an eagerness to investigate the profundities of our own cognizance. An excursion rises above the shallow layers of character and cultural molding, digging into the center of our being where the true self lives. The murmur inside is definitely not a boisterous declaration; rather, a delicate call coaxes us to go past the surface and interface with the substance of who we really are.

The most vital phase in arousing the murmur inside is to develop an act of care. In the rushing about of present day life, we frequently end up trapped in a snare of consistent movement, pretty much ruling out self-reflection. Care gives a safe-haven — a holy space where we can notice our contemplations, feelings, and responses without judgment. It is here of non-critical mindfulness that the murmur inside starts to acquire strength.

As we set out on the excursion of care, we might experience the obstruction of our own personalities. The perpetual jabber, the questions, and the feelings of dread might endeavor to overwhelm the murmur inside. However, with tolerance and tirelessness, we figure out how to calm the commotion and adjust ourselves to the inconspicuous vibrations of our internal voice. The murmur inside, once stirred, turns into a directing light — a compass that guides us towards our real way.

During the time spent self-revelation, we definitely defy the layers of molding that have aggregated throughout the long term. Society, family, instruction — all add to the development of our personality. However, underneath the layers of molding lies the natural substance of our valid selves. Arousing the murmur inside requires a fearless unwinding of these layers, a stripping back of the covers we wear to adjust to outer assumptions.

This excursion of self-revelation isn't without its difficulties. The apprehension about the obscure, the inconvenience of facing stifled feelings, and the protection from change can make internal conflict. However, it is unequivocally at these times of inconvenience that the murmur inside turns out to be more discernible. It is a call to embrace weakness, to stand up to our most profound feelings of trepidation, and to step into the obscure with an open heart.

As we dig further into the openings of our cognizance, we might experience the reverberations of past injuries and injuries. The murmur inside, in any case, isn't a voice of exploitation; it is a voice of flexibility and mending. Recognizing and handling past torment is a basic piece of the excursion, for it is just through acknowledgment and mending that we can completely embrace our legitimate selves.

Chasing arousing the murmur inside, developing self esteem and self-compassion is fundamental. The excursion isn't about flawlessness however about embracing our defects with graciousness and understanding. Self esteem is the salve that mitigates the injuries of self-analysis, permitting the murmur inside to resound with a song of acknowledgment and genuine love.

The outside world frequently besieges us with a bunch of assumptions and meanings of progress. Arousing the murmur inside requires a redefinition of progress — one that is lined up with our most profound qualities and desires. It is an excursion of insight, where we recognize the outside measurements of progress and the inward satisfaction that comes from carrying on with a daily existence consistent with ourselves.

As we adjust our activities to our bona fide values, the murmur inside turns into a directing power, driving us towards an existence of direction and significance. The quest for outside progress might offer brief delight, yet the arrangement with our inward truth brings enduring satisfaction. The murmur inside is a compass that focuses us towards a daily existence that isn't just fruitful by cultural principles yet in addition profoundly significant on an individual level.

During the time spent arousing the murmur inside, we might end up scrutinizing the cultural standards and assumptions that have formed our lives. It is a brave investigation into the validness of our convictions and the qualities that guide our decisions. The murmur inside might rock the boat, encouraging us to manufacture our own way and rethink the importance of an intentional life.

The excursion of self-disclosure is definitely not a lone undertaking; an aggregate arousing swells through our connections and associations with others. As we become more receptive to the murmur inside, we develop a more profound feeling of compassion and understanding for the excursions of people around us. The murmur inside urges us to see others with empathy, perceiving the common humankind that joins every one of us.

In the domain of connections, the murmur inside fills in as a compass for genuineness. It prompts us to convey our necessities and limits with genuineness and weakness. Bona fide associations are produced when we permit the murmur inside to direct us in framing connections that depend on shared regard, understanding, and certified association.

The enlivening of the murmur inside is certainly not a straight interaction; a constant development unfurls as time passes. An excursion of self-revelation welcomes us to embrace the back and forth movement of existence with serenity. The murmur inside trains us to explore the inescapable difficulties and vulnerabilities with elegance and flexibility, realizing that each experience is a venturing stone towards our most noteworthy potential.

In the mission for self-revelation, the murmur inside might lead us to investigate different modalities of self-awareness and profound practices. Whether it be contemplation, care, yoga, or other extraordinary practices, the murmur inside guides us to those modalities that reverberate with our true selves. These practices become a safe-haven — a hallowed space where we can develop our association with the murmur inside.

As the murmur inside acquires strength, it turns into a wellspring of motivation and innovativeness. It is the wellspring of thoughts, bits of knowledge, and developments that arise when we are in arrangement with our valid selves. Imagination, in its most perfect structure, is the outflow of the murmur inside — a novel tune that every individual brings to the orchestra of presence.

The enlivening of the murmur inside isn't bound to the domains of the psyche; it pervades each part of our being, including the actual body. The body is a vessel through which the murmur inside imparts its insight. Through practices, for example, physical mindfulness and careful development, we figure out how to pay attention to the inconspicuous signs of the body, permitting it to be a vehicle for the declaration of our bona fide selves.

In the excursion of self-disclosure, we might experience snapshots of uncertainty and vulnerability. The murmur inside, nonetheless, is an undaunted sidekick — a wellspring of internal realizing that rises above the impediments of the judicious psyche. It is an update that, even despite vulnerability, we can believe the insight that emerges from the profundities of our being.

The murmur inside isn't bound to the domain of the individual; likewise an aggregate power longs for positive change on the planet. As we stir to our own credibility, we become impetuses for change for a bigger scope. The murmur inside moves us to contribute our extraordinary gifts to the improvement of society, making a gradually expanding influence of positive change.

Chasing a significant life, the murmur inside urges us to develop a feeling of appreciation for the current second. Appreciation isn't simply a temporary inclination; it is an approach to being that radiates from a profound appreciation for the extravagance of life. The murmur inside guides us to enjoy the excellence of every second, perceiving that the present is a valuable gift that holds the way in to a satisfying life.

The excursion of enlivening the murmur inside is a long lasting responsibility — a hallowed contract with our credible selves. It's anything but an objective however a nonstop unfurling, a dance between the known and the unexplored world. As we cross the territory of self-disclosure, we become trailblazers of our own inward scene, investigating the unfamiliar regions of the spirit with interest and worship.

In the embroidery of life, the murmur inside is the brilliant string that winds around a story of legitimacy and reason. It is a call to stir from the sleep of congruity and embrace the completion of our being. The murmur inside is the compass that guides us on an excursion of self-revelation, driving us towards a daily existence that isn't just effective by cultural principles yet additionally profoundly significant on an individual level.

The enlivening of the murmur inside is an encouragement to carry on with a day to day existence that is as one with our most profound qualities and yearnings. It is a call to bravely explore the inward scene, defying the shadows and embracing the light inside. As we notice the murmur inside, we leave on an extraordinary excursion — an excursion that rises above the limits of oneself and waves outward, adding to the aggregate arousing of mankind.

1.1 Introduction to the concept of inner strength

The idea of internal strength is a significant and immortal thought that rises above social, verifiable, and individual limits. It is a thought well established in the comprehension that our actual power lies not in outer conditions or actual ability, but rather in the strength, boldness, and grit that exude from the inside. Internal strength is the wellspring of our capacity to explore life's difficulties, go up against affliction, and persist notwithstanding challenges.

At its center, inward strength is a powerful power that dwells in the deepest openings of our being — a wellspring of resolute assurance and an anchor that grounds us in the midst of choppiness. It's anything but a one-size-fits-all idea however a profoundly private and emotional quality that shows exceptionally in every person. The investigation of internal strength includes an excursion into the profundities of our own cognizance, an uncovering of the repository of inward assets that frequently lies lethargic until gathered by life's requests.

One vital part of internal strength is flexibility — the capacity to return from difficulties, affliction, and life's inescapable difficulties. Strength isn't tied in with staying away from challenges or imagining they don't exist; rather, it is turning around them head-on with a soul that will not be broken. It is the ability to adjust, learn, and develop further even with affliction.

Building strength includes developing an outlook that perspectives challenges not as unconquerable hindrances but rather as any open doors for development and self-disclosure.

In the embroidered artwork of life, internal strength additionally winds around the string of mindfulness. Understanding oneself at a profound and legitimate level is a foundation of inward strength. It includes a readiness to investigate the complexities of one's viewpoints, feelings, and convictions with genuineness and receptiveness. Mindfulness is a light that enlightens the shadows inside, permitting us to defy and coordinate parts of ourselves that might have been disregarded or stifled. Through this self-investigation, internal strength arises as one's very own significant comprehension values, reason, and genuine character.

Fortitude is one more indispensable part of internal strength. The power moves us to step outside our usual ranges of familiarity, stand up to fears, and make striking moves lined up with our qualities. Fortitude isn't the shortfall of dread however the capacity to push ahead despite it. The inward fire consumes brilliantly even in the most obscure minutes, directing us through vulnerability and engaging us to pursue decisions that reverberate with our bona fide selves.

An imperative component of inward strength lies in close to home flexibility — the capacity to explore the immense scene of human feelings with beauty and balance. Feelings are an inborn piece of the human experience, and creating internal strength includes developing a sound connection with them. It is tied in with recognizing, understanding, and communicating feelings in a productive way, as opposed to smothering or being overpowered by them. Close to home strength permits us to outfit the extraordinary force of feelings, involving them as impetuses for self-improvement and association with others.

The idea of internal strength is unpredictably attached to the possibility of self-sympathy. In the excursion of life, we frequently experience difficulties, disappointments, and snapshots of weakness. Inward strength doesn't request flawlessness however welcomes us to embrace our defects with generosity and understanding. Self-empathy includes treating oneself with the very warmth and care that one would propose to a dear companion confronting difficulties. It is an emollient for the injuries of self-analysis and a sustaining force that cultivates strength and prosperity.

At its pith, inward strength is a call to credibility — an encouragement to live in arrangement with one's actual self. It requires a profound investigation into individual qualities, convictions, and desires, and a promise to carrying on with a day to day existence that mirrors these internal bits of insight. Credibility isn't an objective however a nonstop excursion of self-revelation and self-articulation. Internal strength is the support point that upholds this excursion, permitting people to explore the intricacies of outer assumptions and cultural standards while remaining consistent with their valid selves.

The development of internal strength is definitely not a single undertaking; it flourishes in the dirt of association and local area. People are innately friendly animals, and the help of significant connections assumes a crucial part in the improvement of inward strength. Sharing our difficulties, looking for help, and offering backing to others make an embroidery of interconnected strength. In the texture of local area, people track down comfort, consolation, and the common thinking that adds to the aggregate supply of internal strength.

Otherworldliness is another aspect that converges with the idea of inward strength. Notwithstanding strict affiliations, otherworldliness includes an association with an option that could be more significant than oneself — a wellspring of importance, reason, and greatness. Internal strength frequently draws from this profound well, furnishing people with a feeling of direction and a system for exploring life's vulnerabilities. It is an update that, in the midst of the recurring pattern of day to day existence, there exists a more profound, getting through aspect that can act as a directing light.

The improvement of internal strength is definitely not a direct interaction however a recurrent and iterative excursion. It requires continuous self-reflection, a readiness to gain from encounters, and the lowliness to embrace change. Inward strength is definitely not a static characteristic however a powerful quality that develops over the long haul, acquiring profundity and wealth through the times of life. It is a long lasting obligation to self-revelation, development, and the consistent unfurling of one's true capacity.

In the cutting edge world, where outside accomplishments and material achievement frequently become the overwhelming focus, the idea of inward strength fills in as a sign of the significant supply of force inside every person. It challenges the idea that strength is exclusively estimated by outer achievements and supports a change in center towards the development of internal characteristics. Inward strength isn't a dismissal of outside progress yet an affirmation that genuine versatility and satisfaction emerge from a groundwork of internal prosperity.

The investigation of internal strength welcomes people to participate in rehearses that feed the psyche, body, and soul. These practices might incorporate care and reflection, which develop present-second mindfulness and a feeling of internal quiet. Proactive tasks that advance wellbeing and essentialness add to the encapsulation of solidarity. Innovative pursuits and self-articulation become channels through which internal strength tracks down outward appearance. The joining of these practices into day to day existence cultivates a comprehensive way to deal with internal prosperity.

In the instructive domain, the idea of internal strength holds monstrous importance. Conventional instruction frequently focuses on the procurement of information and outer accomplishments. While these are without a doubt significant, the development of internal strength adds an element of the capacity to understand people on a profound level, versatility, and mindfulness to the instructive scene.

Teachers assume a pivotal part in cultivating a climate that urges understudies to investigate and foster their inward assets, setting them up for scholastic accomplishment as well as for the intricacies of life past the homeroom.

In the work environment, the idea of inward strength has extraordinary ramifications for authoritative culture and administration. A working environment that qualities and sustains the inward prosperity of its representatives encourages a culture of cooperation, development, and flexibility. Pioneers who encapsulate inward strength motivate and engage their groups, making a tough and high-performing hierarchical ethos. The acknowledgment of the interaction between inward strength and expert achievement makes ready for a more comprehensive and maintainable way to deal with vocation improvement.

As social orders wrestle with difficulties going from natural emergencies to social disparities, the idea of inward strength arises as an impetus for positive change. People with internal strength are bound to add to the prosperity of their networks, participate in selfless activities, and promoter for civil rights. The aggregate development of inward strength turns into a main impetus for cultural flexibility and change.

All in all, the idea of inward strength is a diverse and dynamic investigation into the profundities of human potential. It envelops strength, mindfulness, fortitude, the capacity to understand people at their core, and validness. The excursion of creating inward strength is a deep rooted try that unfurls through self-reflection, association with others, and the combination of practices that sustain the psyche, body, and soul. In a world that frequently underlines outside accomplishments, the acknowledgment of inward strength fills in as a strong update that genuine flexibility, satisfaction, and prosperity emerge from the profound well inside every person.

1.2 Personal anecdotes or stories illustrating the power of inner strength

In the embroidery of human experience, individual tales and stories act as striking strings that weave the account of inward strength. These accounts, frequently well established in the texture of individual lives, enlighten the extraordinary power that arises when internal versatility, boldness, and grit are called despite difficulties. Such stories are stories of win as well as windows into the actual pith of the human soul — a soul that can transcend misfortune, explore vulnerability, and arise more grounded on the opposite side.

Consider the narrative of Emily, a young lady who confronted the overwhelming test of reconstructing her life after an unexpected and surprising misfortune. Emily's process was set apart by sorrow, vulnerability, and the need to reclassify her healthy identity. In the profundities of her distress, she found an internal strength that turned into the foundation of her flexibility. It wasn't necessary to focus on deleting the aggravation yet about recognizing it, believing it profoundly, and permitting it to be an impetus for development.

Through treatment, support from friends and family, and her own unfaltering assurance, Emily tracked down a significant well of solidarity inside herself. Her story is a demonstration of the extraordinary force of inward strength in exploring the intricacies of misfortune and reconstructing an existence with recently discovered reason.

Another strong story unfurls in the existence of Alex, an expert competitor whose vocation was suddenly hindered by a weakening injury. The way to recuperation was about actual restoration as well as a significant excursion into the profundities of inward strength. Alex confronted the test of rethinking his personality past the domain of sports. It was a cycle that necessary actual perseverance as well as a resolute outlook to defy misfortunes and drive forward through the exhausting recovery process.

Through reflection, appreciation rehearses, and the development of mental versatility, Alex recuperated as well as arisen with a reinforced identity. His story epitomizes how internal strength, when outfit, can change difficulties into open doors for self-awareness and self-disclosure.

The story of Maya, a single parent exploring the intricacies of life as a parent and a requesting profession, gives one more focal point through which the force of internal strength becomes clear. Maya confronted the everyday shuffle of adjusting work, nurturing, and taking care of oneself, frequently feeling the heaviness of cultural assumptions and individual questions. Amidst the disarray, she found that her inward strength was not tied in with accomplishing an ideal equilibrium but rather about embracing flaws and figuring out how to focus on what really made a difference. Maya's excursion of self-empathy, flexibility, and validness is a reference point for those exploring the perplexing dance of current life, exhibiting how internal strength can bloom in the midst of the difficulties of regular presence.

These individual stories highlight the comprehensiveness of the human experience while featuring the special manners by which people tap into their internal supplies of solidarity. They are updates that strength isn't generally tracked down in great signals however frequently in the peaceful snapshots of self-reflection, weakness, and the decision to persist despite difficulty.

Consider the story of James, a moderately aged proficient who ended up at a junction in his vocation. Confronted with the possibility of progress and vulnerability, James wrestled with dread and self-question. However, at this time of emergency, he found a startling wellspring of mental fortitude inside himself. James chose to embrace the chance for rehash, inclining toward uneasiness and venturing outside the bounds of his usual range of familiarity. The interaction was not without challenges, but rather through contemplation, flexibility, and a readiness to defy his own restricting convictions, James explored the profession change effectively as well as uncovered a recharged feeling of direction and enthusiasm. His story represents how inward strength can engage people to explore urgent snapshots of progress and change.

The story of Sarah, an understudy confronting scholastic difficulties, gives one more impactful representation of the force of inward strength. Sarah experienced challenges in her examinations, and the strain to live up to cultural assumptions weighed vigorously on her. Rather than surrendering to the apprehension about disappointment, Sarah took advantage of her internal versatility. Through a blend of steadiness, looking for help when required, and rethinking her mentality, she changed her scholarly excursion. Sarah's story fills in as an update that inward strength isn't about the shortfall of moves however about the ability to defy them sincerely, versatility, and a development situated mentality.

In the corporate world, the story of David, a pioneer exploring an unpredictable business climate, reveals insight into how internal strength turns into a directing power in authority. Confronted with hierarchical difficulties, David perceived that genuine initiative included key discernment as well as a profound well of inward versatility. Through snapshots of vulnerability, difficult independent direction, and the obligation of driving a group, David improved his skill to remain focused and lead with realness. His story epitomizes how inward strength is a vital resource in administration, empowering people to control through difficulties with elegance, courage, and an emphasis on encouraging a strong hierarchical culture.

The accounts of Emily, Alex, Maya, James, Sarah, and David on the whole represent that the force of internal strength rises above age, orientation, and expert foundations. A general power can be outfit by anybody ready to set out on the excursion of self-revelation and versatility. These stories likewise disperse the legend that inward strength is a proper characteristic; all things considered, they depict it as a dynamic and developing quality that can be developed and reinforced through cognizant exertion and a promise to self-awareness.

The repetitive topic across these tales is the job of reflection in opening inward strength. Every individual confronted a snapshot of retribution — a potential chance to dive into their own internal scenes, stand up to weaknesses, and saddle their inborn versatility. This course of self-investigation frequently elaborate looking for help from others, whether through treatment, mentorship, or significant associations with loved ones. The interconnectedness of human encounters is apparent in the aggregate help that these people got, accentuating the job of local area and association in the development of inward strength.

Besides, these accounts stress the significance of reexamining difficulties as any open doors for development. Inward strength isn't tied in with keeping away from challenges however about changing them into impetuses for positive change. Whether it's the passing of a friend or family member, a lifelong mishap, scholastic battles, or the intricacies of nurturing, each challenge turned into a cauldron where people found the flexibility, fortitude, and credibility inside themselves. This groundbreaking viewpoint welcomes a change in mentality — from review impediments as unconquerable hindrances to remembering them as venturing stones on the excursion of individual development.

The idea of internal strength additionally crosses with the thought of weakness. Every story reflects snapshots of weakness — times when people confronted vulnerability, dread, or self-question. Oddly, it is at these times of weakness that internal strength sparkles most splendidly. By embracing weakness, people open themselves to the lavishness of the human experience, considering genuine association with oneself as well as other people. The eagerness to be powerless turns into a wellspring of solidarity, encouraging versatility and developing the comprehension of one's own abilities.

Additionally, these accounts challenge the cultural story that strength is inseparable from apathy or the concealment of feelings. In actuality, the force of inward strength lies in the affirmation and real articulation of feelings. Whether it's the sadness felt by Emily, the dissatisfaction experienced by Alex, or oneself uncertainty faced by Maya, every inclination turned into a guidepost on the excursion toward inward strength.

The ability to explore and coordinate a range of feelings adds to close to home versatility — a principal part of internal strength.

In the more extensive setting of cultural assumptions and social standards, these stories represent the fortitude to resist outer meanings of achievement and strength. Maya's story, for example, challenges the ordinary account of "having everything" and features the significance of focusing on one's prosperity and credibility over cultural assumptions. Likewise, James' process resists the idea that vocation advances ought to be driven exclusively by outer measurements of progress, accentuating the characteristic benefit of adjusting one's expert life to individual reason.

These individual accounts likewise underline the interconnectedness of various components of internal strength. Versatility, mental fortitude, mindfulness, the capacity to understand people on a deeper level, and legitimacy are not detached qualities but rather features of a comprehensive and coordinated idea. The development of internal strength includes an agreeable improvement of these aspects, making a synergistic impact that intensifies a singular's capacity to explore life's intricacies.

Basically, these individual stories act as living tributes to the groundbreaking force of inward strength. They enlighten the way of self-revelation, versatility, and realness that people can leave upon when confronted with difficulties. These stories reverberate as encouraging signs and motivation, advising us that, inside the center of our being, lies a monstrous supply of solidarity ready to be uncovered. From the perspective of these individual tales, the idea of internal strength arises not as a theoretical thought but rather as a lived insight — a demonstration of the uncommon limit of the human.

1.3 Overview of the journey ahead and the importance of listening to the whispers within

Leaving on the excursion of self-revelation and internal investigation is much the same as heading out on an immense and strange sea. The way forward is both elating and overwhelming, set apart by the commitment of self-revelation, self-awareness, and the disclosing of one's legitimate self. As we explore this excursion, it becomes basic to perceive the significance of paying attention to the murmurs inside — the unobtrusive, frequently disregarded, yet significantly savvy murmurings of our internal identities. These murmurs are the compass that guides us through the intricacies of life, guiding us towards credibility, reason, and a more profound association with our most genuine pith.

The excursion ahead is definitely not a straight direction however a winding and dynamic investigation into the profundities of our cognizance. It welcomes us to strip back the layers of cultural molding, outside assumptions, and deliberate limits to uncover the crude and bona fide self that dwells underneath. In this course of self-revelation, we experience the reverberations of our past, the shadows that shape our present, and the endless conceivable outcomes that unfurl in the material of our future.

At the core of this excursion lies the idea of internal strength — a wellspring of flexibility, mental fortitude, and genuineness that turns into the directing power through the recurring pattern of life. Internal strength is certainly not a decent characteristic yet a unique quality that develops and extends as we draw in with the different features of our reality. The resolute sidekick enables us to go up against difficulties, embrace weakness, and explore the intricacies of connections, work, and self-improvement.

The murmurs inside, frequently overwhelmed by the clamor of outer impacts, cultural assumptions, and the buzzing about of day to day existence, act as the compass of inward strength. These murmurs manifest in the tranquil snapshots of thoughtfulness, the bumps of instinct, and the unpretentious pulls at our souls. Paying attention to these murmurs requires an intentional dialing back, an eagerness to be available, and a receptiveness to the insight that emerges from the inside.

The significance of standing by listening to the murmurs inside lies in the significant direction they offer in exploring life's junction. In a world that frequently barrages us with outside improvements, cultural standards, and the strain to adjust, the murmurs inside become a wellspring of realness. They guide us towards decisions lined up with our qualities, yearnings, and the genuine pith of what our identity is. At the point when we regard these murmurs, we leave on an excursion that rises above the quest for outer achievement and lines up with a more profound, more significant presence.

The murmurs inside additionally hold the way to opening our undiscovered capacity. As we stand by listening to these unpretentious signals, we get to the repository of inventiveness, knowledge, and development that lives inside our cognizance. The murmurs are the dream that moves our remarkable articulation, whether it be in our work, connections, or imaginative undertakings. At the point when we honor these murmurs, we tap into the wellspring of our inventive power, contributing a special song to the orchestra of life.

Additionally, paying attention to the murmurs inside is a fundamental practice for developing mindfulness. At the times of calm reflection, we become receptive to the subtleties of our viewpoints, feelings, and convictions. This uplifted mindfulness permits us to recognize the examples that shape our way of behaving, the molding that impacts our decisions, and the valid longings that stew underneath the surface. Through this interaction, we gain clearness on what our identity is and the main thing to us, empowering a more deliberate and intentional approach to everyday life.

The murmurs inside likewise act as couriers of instinct — a quiet yet strong direction framework that rises above levelheaded idea. Instinct is the intrinsic insight that emerges from the profundities of our being, offering bits of knowledge past the impediments of rationale and investigation. At the point when we pay attention to the murmurs inside, we tap into this instinctive insight, permitting it to illuminate our choices, guide our activities, and explore the obscure with a feeling of trust and internal knowing.

The excursion ahead, directed by the murmurs inside, welcomes us to embrace weakness as a passage to validness. It is a call to face the shadows, the unsettled feelings, and the parts of ourselves that might have been covered up or dismissed. Through this gutsy investigation, we unwind the layers that dark our actual selves, permitting the murmurs inside to turn into an ensemble of self-acknowledgment and confidence.

During the time spent paying attention to the murmurs inside, we additionally experience the groundbreaking force of strength. Life, by its inclination, presents difficulties, misfortunes, and snapshots of vulnerability. Inward strength, invigorated by the murmurs inside, enables us to confront affliction with beauty and assurance. It is the comprehension that versatility isn't the shortfall of moves however the ability to rise, adjust, and develop further despite them. The murmurs inside become a consistent buddy in exploring the tempests of life, offering comfort, direction, and a sign of our inborn strength.

The murmurs inside entice us to embrace the idea of careful living — a condition of present-second mindfulness that rises above the unending babble of the brain. Care is the act of being completely present, noticing our contemplations and feelings without judgment, and developing a profound association with the current second. At the point when we participate in careful living, we make space to hear the murmurs inside, to pay attention to the nuances of our inward scene, and to answer existence with lucidity and aim.

Moreover, the significance of paying attention to the murmurs inside reaches out to the domain of connections. Credible associations with others are supported when we are sensitive to our own internal truth. The murmurs guide us in communicating our necessities, defining limits, and participating in connections that line up with our qualities. At the point when people in a relationship pay attention to their particular murmurs inside, they make a space for common development, understanding, and credible association.

The excursion of paying attention to the murmurs inside is certainly not a singular undertaking; an aggregate arousing swells through networks, associations, and social orders. As people participate in this inward investigation, they add to an aggregate shift — a development towards a more cognizant, merciful, and credible approach to being. The murmurs inside become an aggregate song, fitting the yearnings of people with the more extensive embroidery of mankind.

With regards to administration, the significance of paying attention to the murmurs inside becomes fundamental. Pioneers who are sensitive to their inward direction are better prepared to explore the intricacies of navigation, move their groups, and cultivate a culture of legitimacy and development. Initiative, directed by the murmurs inside, rises above the customary standards of power and control, embracing a more comprehensive and humane methodology.

The murmurs inside are likewise a call to ecological cognizance — a sign of our interconnectedness with the regular world. As people stand by listening to their internal direction, they become mindful of the effect of their decisions on the climate, cultivating a feeling of obligation and stewardship. This environmental mindfulness, directed by the murmurs inside, adds to a more manageable and amicable relationship with the planet.

As we set out on the excursion ahead, it is fundamental to perceive that paying attention to the murmurs inside is definitely not a one-time try however a consistent practice. The murmurs might be unobtrusive, handily overwhelmed by the commotion of outside impacts, everyday obligations, and the requests of a speedy world. Developing the specialty of listening requires responsibility, persistence, and a readiness to make snapshots of tranquility in the midst of the rushing about of life.

In the excursion ahead, there will be snapshots of uneasiness and vulnerability. The murmurs inside might direct us to defy parts of ourselves that we would prefer to keep away from, or they might push us to go with decisions that rock the boat. It is definitively at these times of uneasiness that the murmurs inside gain strength. They become a wellspring of fortitude, empowering us to step into the obscure, embrace weakness, and trust the unfurling of our special process.

The murmurs inside are not restricted to snapshots of reflection or contemplation; they manifest in the common snapshots of day to day existence. Whether it's the delicate poke to seek after an energy, the natural sense that a specific choice feels right, or the internal realizing that a relationship is lined up with our bona fide self — these are murmurs that guide our way. Figuring out how to perceive and believe these murmurs amidst regular daily existence is a fundamental part of the excursion ahead.

The excursion of paying attention to the murmurs inside likewise welcomes us to develop a feeling of appreciation. Appreciation is the act of recognizing and valuing the overflow present in our lives. At the point when we approach existence with a thankful heart, we make a broad space for the murmurs inside to be heard. Appreciation turns into an extension between the internal and external universes, cultivating a profound appreciation for the current second and the open doors for development and association that life presents.

All in all, the excursion ahead is a significant investigation into the domains of self-revelation, validness, and inward strength. Paying attention to the murmurs inside isn't simply an individual practice yet an extraordinary pathway that rises above the person to add to the aggregate arousing of mankind. It is a call to embrace weakness, develop flexibility, and live with careful aim. As we notice the murmurs inside, we set out on an excursion that uncovers the extravagance of the human soul — an excursion towards a day to day existence that resounds with validness, reason.

In the ensemble of life, in the midst of the chaos of outside impacts, assumptions, and the hurrying around of day to day presence, lies an unpretentious yet powerful song — the murmurs inside. These murmurs, frequently overwhelmed by the commotion of the outside world, convey the significant insight of our internal identities. The significance of paying attention to these murmurs inside couldn't possibly be more significant, as they act as a directing compass on the excursion of self-revelation, realness, and self-awareness.

At the core of this importance is the acknowledgment that the murmurs inside exude from the most profound openings of our being. They are not transitory contemplations or passing feelings but rather significant messages from the center of our legitimate selves. In a world that frequently pulls us in heap headings, these murmurs act as a relentless anchor, helping us to remember our actual embodiment and directing us towards decisions that line up with our qualities, desires, and inward insights.

One key part of paying attention to the murmurs inside is the development of mindfulness. The murmurs convey the nuanced bits of knowledge into our viewpoints, feelings, and convictions, offering a mirror into the complexities of our internal scene.

Through careful regard for these murmurs, we gain clearness on the examples that shape our ways of behaving, the molding that impacts our decisions, and the true cravings that stew underneath the surface. This uplifted mindfulness turns into a foundation for purposeful living, empowering us to explore existence with a more profound comprehension of ourselves.

Besides, the murmurs inside go about as couriers of instinct — a quiet yet intense power that rises above reasonable idea. Instinct is the inborn insight that emerges from the profundities of our being, offering experiences past the restrictions of rationale and investigation. At the point when we stand by listening to these murmurs, we tap into this natural knowledge, permitting it to illuminate our choices, guide our activities, and explore the obscure with a feeling of trust and internal knowing. In a world that frequently focuses on outside approval and information driven direction, the significance of respecting our instinct turns into a strong cure, driving us towards decisions that resound with our credible selves.

The meaning of paying attention to the murmurs inside stretches out to the domain of validness. In a general public that much of the time supports similarity and the adherence to cultural standards, these murmurs become the voice of our most genuine selves. They guide us towards decisions that mirror our extraordinary character, values, and desires. Valid living includes adjusting our outer activities to our inner insights, and the murmurs inside go about as a steady suggestion to embrace and communicate our credibility in each feature of life.

Moreover, the murmurs inside hold the way to opening our undiscovered possibility. They act as a wellspring of inventiveness, development, and understanding that lives inside our cognizance. At the point when we adjust ourselves to these murmurs, we get sufficiently close to the repository of thoughts, gifts, and potential outcomes that might have been neglected or misjudged. The murmurs become the dream that moves our exceptional articulation, whether it be in our work, connections, or imaginative undertakings. The significance of noticing these murmurs lies in the groundbreaking power they hold to release our imaginative potential and contribute our special gifts to the world.

Paying attention to the murmurs inside is likewise an act of developing flexibility — a fundamental quality for exploring the unavoidable difficulties and vulnerabilities of life. The murmurs become a wellspring of inward strength, directing us to confront misfortune with effortlessness and assurance. Strength, in this unique situation, isn't the shortfall of moves however the ability to rise, adjust, and develop further despite them. The murmurs inside become a consistent friend in exploring the tempests of life, offering comfort, direction, and a sign of our inborn strength.

With regards to independent direction, the significance of paying attention to the murmurs inside becomes clear. Decisions that line up with our valid selves are bound to prompt a feeling of satisfaction and prosperity.

The murmurs act as an ethical compass, guiding us towards choices that reverberate with our qualities and add to our general feeling of direction. In snapshots of vulnerability or junction, these murmurs become a wellspring of direction, assisting us with knowing the way that lines up with our most genuine expectations.

The excursion of paying attention to the murmurs inside is likewise a call to embrace weakness — a passage to genuineness and more profound association. The murmurs frequently guide us to stand up to parts of ourselves that might be awkward or expect mental fortitude to investigate. By embracing weakness, we open ourselves to the lavishness of the human experience, considering legitimate association with ourselves as well as other people. It is in these weak minutes that the murmurs inside become a melody of self-acknowledgment and self esteem.

In addition, the significance of paying attention to the murmurs inside stretches out to the domain of connections. Genuine associations with others are sustained when we are receptive to our own inward truth. The murmurs guide us in communicating our necessities, defining limits, and taking part in connections that line up with our qualities. At the point when people in a relationship pay attention to their particular murmurs inside, they make a space for shared development, understanding, and legitimate association. With regards to organizations, companionships, and relational peculiarities, the murmurs become a scaffold for open correspondence, encouraging profound and significant associations.

The murmurs inside are likewise a call to ecological cognizance — an indication of our interconnectedness with the regular world. As people stand by listening to their internal direction, they become mindful of the effect of their decisions on the climate, cultivating a feeling of obligation and stewardship. This natural mindfulness, directed by the murmurs inside, adds to a more economical and agreeable relationship with the planet. The murmurs become a suggestion to live as one with the Earth, perceiving that our singular activities have expanding influences on the aggregate prosperity of the planet.

With regards to authority, the significance of paying attention to the murmurs inside can't be put into words. Pioneers who are receptive to their internal direction are better prepared to explore the intricacies of navigation, motivate their groups, and encourage a culture of legitimacy and development. Initiative, directed by the murmurs inside, rises above the customary standards of power and control, embracing a more comprehensive and merciful methodology. Pioneers who regard the murmurs become guides of genuineness, establishing conditions that empower the individual and expert development of their groups.

The excursion of paying attention to the murmurs inside is definitely not a lone undertaking; an aggregate arousing swells through networks, associations, and social orders. As people participate in this internal investigation, they add to an aggregate shift — a development towards a more cognizant, empathetic, and real approach to being.

The murmurs inside become an aggregate tune, orchestrating the goals of people with the more extensive embroidery of humankind. This aggregate arousing can possibly catalyze positive change, at the singular level as well as in the texture of cultural standards and social ideal models.

As we leave on the excursion of paying attention to the murmurs inside, it is fundamental to perceive that this training is certainly not a one-time occasion yet a ceaseless and developing cycle. The murmurs might be unobtrusive, handily overwhelmed by the commotion of outside impacts, everyday obligations, and the requests of a speedy world. Developing the specialty of listening requires responsibility, persistence, and an eagerness to make snapshots of tranquility in the midst of the rushing about of life.

In the excursion ahead, there will be snapshots of uneasiness and vulnerability. The murmurs inside might direct us to defy parts of ourselves that we would prefer to stay away from, or they might prod us to go with decisions that rock the boat. It is unequivocally at these times of inconvenience that the murmurs inside gain strength. They become a wellspring of mental fortitude, empowering us to step into the obscure, embrace weakness, and trust the unfurling of our one of a kind excursion.

The murmurs inside are not bound to snapshots of reflection or contemplation; they manifest in the standard snapshots of day to day existence. Whether it's the delicate poke to seek after an enthusiasm, the natural sense that a specific choice feels right, or the inward realizing that a relationship is lined up with our bona fide self — these are murmurs that guide our way. Figuring out how to perceive and believe these murmurs amidst regular daily existence is an indispensable part of the excursion ahead.

Chapter 2

Embracing Vulnerability

Embracing weakness is a significant excursion that takes us through the profundities of our own mankind. It is a valiant demonstration of freeing ourselves up to the full range of feelings and encounters that make us what our identity is. In a world that frequently praises strength and versatility, weakness is much of the time misjudged or even excused as a shortcoming. Notwithstanding, it is in embracing our weakness that we find the genuine substance of our being and interface with others on a more profound level.

At its center, weakness is about realness and the eagerness to appear as we are, defects what not. It requires a cognizant decision to relinquish the covers we wear to safeguard ourselves from judgment or dismissal. All things considered, it welcomes us to be crude and genuine, recognizing our apprehensions, instabilities, and vulnerabilities. In doing as such, we make the way for certifiable associations, both with ourselves and with everyone around us.

Brene Brown, a famous scientist and narrator, has gone through years concentrating on weakness and its effect on human association. In her momentous work, she characterizes weakness as "vulnerability, risk, and profound openness." It is the readiness to step into the obscure, to face challenges, and to be seen without the wellbeing nets of flawlessness or resistance. Earthy colored contends that weakness is definitely not an indication of shortcoming yet rather the origin of mental fortitude, imagination, and significant associations.

In a general public that frequently puts a top notch on areas of strength for seeming set up, weakness can be a progressive demonstration. It challenges the overall account that compares weakness with delicacy and difficulties the idea that strength is inseparable from a shortfall of weakness. All things considered, embracing weakness requires a redefinition of solidarity — one that perceives the strength and boldness it takes to be open, legit, and bona fide in a world that may not necessarily in all cases embrace these characteristics.

To comprehend weakness, investigating its underlying foundations in our initial encounters and social conditioning is fundamental. Since early on, a large number of us are instructed to conceal our weaknesses, to act courageously in any event, when we are harming inside. Society frequently sends us messages that weakness is an obligation, something to be kept away from no matter what. This cultural molding can lead us to construct profound walls, disguising our actual selves trying to squeeze into predefined molds of adequacy.

Notwithstanding, the expense of this profound protection is steep. While it might safeguard us from the apparent risks of being powerless, it likewise disengages us from our real selves as well as other people. It makes a hindrance that forestalls profound and significant associations, letting us feeling disconnected and be. The feeling of dread toward weakness can appear as an anxiety toward dismissal, judgment, or disparagement, and it very well may be a strong power that shapes our way of behaving and decisions.

In connections, weakness is in many cases the paste that ties individuals together. It cultivates closeness and trust, making a space where people can be genuinely recognized the truth about and acknowledged. At the point when we permit ourselves to be powerless, we welcome others to do likewise, making a complementary trade of transparency and realness. This correspondence frames the groundwork of sound and satisfying connections, whether they be heartfelt, familial, or non-romantic.

However, embracing weakness is certainly not a one-time occasion; a continuous practice requires mindfulness and self-empathy. It includes an eagerness to constantly strip back the layers of self-security and stand up to the uneasiness that accompanies uncovering our actual selves. This interaction is generally difficult, as it requires defying our most profound apprehensions and weaknesses. It includes recognizing that flawlessness is a deception and that our value isn't dependent upon our capacity to satisfy ridiculous guidelines.

One of the critical parts of weakness is its convergence with disgrace. Disgrace, as characterized by Brown, is the strongly excruciating inclination that we are contemptible of affection and having a place. A strong power drives us to conceal our weaknesses, expecting that in the event that others see our actual selves, they will dismiss us. Disgrace flourishes in mystery and quiet, making weakness a strong remedy. At the point when we focus a light on our weaknesses and offer them with others, we decrease the force of disgrace and make space for sympathy and association.

The oddity of weakness is that while it requires an eagerness to uncover our flaws, there's no need to focus on looking for approval or endorsement from others. All things considered, it is tied in with developing a profound identity worth and acknowledgment. At the point when we embrace weakness, we avow that our value is intrinsic and doesn't rely upon outer decisions. This change in context permits us to step into our realness with a feeling of strengthening, liberated from the shackles of cultural assumptions.

In the work environment, weakness can change authoritative societies and administration styles. Customary ideas of initiative frequently stress an emotionless and unflappable disposition, however this approach can make a culture of dread and progressive system. Pioneers who embrace weakness make a more comprehensive and imaginative workplace. At the point when pioneers will concede botches, face challenges, and show their credible selves, it establishes a vibe that supports transparency and inventiveness among colleagues.

The force of weakness in administration is clear in the idea of "worker authority," where pioneers focus on the prosperity and development of their colleagues. This style of initiative requires a serious level of weakness, as it includes conceding impediments, looking for criticism, and encouraging a culture of cooperation. At the point when pioneers model weakness, it makes a far reaching influence all through the association, cultivating a culture where people feel engaged to carry their entire selves to work.

In any case, the excursion of embracing weakness isn't without its difficulties. The apprehension about judgment and dismissal can be profoundly imbued, requiring purposeful and predictable work to survive. It might include standing up to past injuries or cultural molding that have formed our relationship with weakness. Looking for help from specialists, mentors, or care groups can be priceless in exploring this excursion, giving a place of refuge to investigate and communicate our weaknesses.

Developing self-sympathy is one more essential part of embracing weakness. Self-sympathy includes treating ourselves with the very benevolence and understanding that we would propose to a companion confronting comparative difficulties. It requires recognizing that being human means being blemished and that weakness is an innate piece of the human experience. Creating self-sympathy permits us to move toward weakness with a tenderness that works with development and recuperating.

The social and cultural setting where we reside likewise assumes a critical part in molding our relationship with weakness. Various societies might have differing perspectives toward transparency and weakness, impacting individual discernments and ways of behaving. In certain societies, the accentuation on aggregate character and association might make weakness all the more socially adequate, while in others, independence and confidence might make obstructions to communicating weakness.

Lately, there has been a developing acknowledgment of the significance of psychological well-being and prosperity, adding to a change in cultural mentalities toward weakness. Developments pushing for realness, for example, the body inspiration development and the destigmatization of emotional wellness issues, are testing ordinary ideas of flawlessness and strength. These social movements make space for people to embrace weakness without the apprehension about being judged or underestimated.

The computerized age plays likewise had an impact in reshaping the elements of weakness. Virtual entertainment stages give a stage to people to share their valid selves, cultivating a feeling of local area and association. Be that as it may, the organized idea of online entertainment can likewise add to a mutilated feeling of the real world, as people might contrast their in the background and others' feature reels. Exploring the computerized scene requires an insightful eye and a cognizant work to develop bona fide associations past the surface level.

In the domain of imagination, weakness is the soul of development and creativity. Inventiveness frequently includes pushing limits, facing challenges, and embracing the vulnerability of the innovative strategy. At the point when specialists, essayists, and makers permit themselves to be powerless, they tap into a wellspring of motivation and validness. The eagerness to communicate their one of a kind viewpoints and encounters adds wealth to their work, reverberating with crowds on a profound and instinctive level.

The anxiety toward weakness can be especially articulated in imaginative pursuits, as the demonstration of sharing one's manifestations can want to uncover the deepest layers of oneself. Defeating this dread requires a change in outlook, seeing weakness not as a danger but rather as a wellspring of solidarity. Imagination flourishes in the fruitful soil of weakness, and the most convincing works frequently arise when makers will wander into the unknown domain of their own validness.

In the domain of schooling, encouraging a culture of weakness can improve the growth opportunity for understudies. At the point when instructors model weakness by recognizing their own errors and vulnerabilities, it makes a place of refuge for understudies to get clarification on some pressing issues, offer their viewpoints, and face scholarly challenges. A homeroom that embraces weakness turns into a unique climate where interest and investigation are empowered, laying the preparation for a long lasting adoration for learning.

Guardians, as well, assume a critical part in forming their youngsters' relationship with weakness. By establishing a climate where feelings are recognized and communicated, guardians can show their kids that weakness is a characteristic and fundamental piece of the human experience. Empowering open correspondence and approving youngsters' sentiments encourages the capacity to appreciate people on a deeper level and flexibility. At the point when youngsters discover that it is protected to be powerless, they foster an identity worth that isn't dependent upon outside approval.

The crossing point of weakness and versatility is a strong and nuanced one. While weakness is frequently connected with transparency and openness, versatility is the ability to return from difficulties and difficulty. Perplexingly, embracing weakness is a critical part of building versatility. At the point when we permit ourselves to be defenseless, we foster a more noteworthy ability to adjust and explore life's unavoidable highs and lows. Strength isn't tied in with staying away from weakness yet turning around it with mental fortitude and a development outlook.

Care rehearses, like contemplation and self-reflection, can be significant devices in the excursion of embracing weakness. These practices develop mindfulness and presence, permitting people to notice their considerations and feelings without judgment. Care empowers a profound investigation of oneself, revealing layers of weakness that might have been covered underneath the surface. It gives an establishment to self-sympathy and a more prominent comprehension of the interconnectedness, everything being equal.

The connection among weakness and sympathy is harmonious. Sympathy, the capacity to comprehend and talk about the thoughts of another, is increased when people embrace their own weakness. At the point when we perceive and acknowledge our own battles, it extends our ability to identify with the battles of others. This common human experience makes obligations of understanding and empathy, encouraging a feeling of association that rises above individual contrasts.

Be that as it may, sympathy requires undivided attention and an eagerness to be available with others in their weakness. It includes saving decisions and assumptions, making space for others to genuinely put themselves out there. In a world that frequently esteems handy solutions and arrangements, the endowment of sympathetic listening is an uncommon and valuable one. It conveys to others that their encounters matter, and their weakness is met with understanding and backing.

The job of weakness in the mending system is significant. Whether mending from past injuries, exploring despondency, or tending to psychological wellness challenges, embracing weakness is an extraordinary power. In restorative settings, weakness frames the bedrock of the remedial relationship. At the point when people have a good sense of security to share their most profound feelings of trepidation and weaknesses, it makes a space for mending and development. The remedial interaction itself is an excursion of weakness, as people stand up to and make significance of their encounters.

Despite fundamental difficulties, weakness turns into an impetus for social change. Developments upholding for equity, uniformity, and basic freedoms frequently start with people and networks embracing their weakness. At the point when individuals will share their accounts, face fundamental treacheries, and support what they have faith in, it ignites an aggregate development toward positive change. Weakness notwithstanding misfortune turns into an amazing asset for destroying severe frameworks and cultivating a more impartial society.

As we explore the intricacies of embracing weakness, it is fundamental to perceive that weakness isn't inseparable from naivety or detachment. There's no need to focus on presenting ourselves wildly to mischief or surrendering solid limits. All things considered, it is a cognizant decision to be open and genuine while keeping a healthy identity regard and insight. Embracing weakness includes defining limits that safeguard our prosperity while considering real association and development.

2.1 Exploring the connection between vulnerability and inner strength

Investigating the multifaceted association among weakness and internal strength discloses a significant exchange of human feelings and flexibility. From the outset, weakness and internal strength might seem like restricting powers — one related with receptiveness and the other with mettle. In any case, a more profound investigation uncovers that they are unpredictably woven into the texture of our close to home and mental prosperity.

Weakness, frequently saw as a condition of openness and receptiveness to likely mischief, is, as a matter of fact, a door to credible self-articulation. It requires a readiness to embrace our defects, fears, and vulnerabilities, permitting us to interface with our actual selves. A long way from being an indication of shortcoming, weakness turns into the establishment whereupon inward strength is fabricated. It is the affirmation and acknowledgment of our weaknesses that engages us to explore life's difficulties with versatility and boldness.

Notwithstanding misfortune, the ability to be powerless turns into a wellspring of internal strength. At the point when we permit ourselves to be found in our snapshots of battle, we tap into a well of validness that encourages real associations with others. It is through weakness that we welcome sympathy and backing, making an organization of profound bonds that add to our inward strength. The demonstration of sharing our weaknesses interfaces us with others as well as fills in as our very own demonstration self-acknowledgment and strength.

Brene Brown, a specialist prestigious for her work on weakness, stresses that weakness is certainly not an indication of delicacy yet rather the origin of boldness. It takes fortitude to confront the vulnerabilities of life, to defy our feelings of dread, and to remain in our reality. This mental fortitude is the embodiment of internal strength — a steady power that rises up out of the profundities of weakness. In the weakness, we track down the solidarity to drive forward, to adjust, and to develop.

The excursion of investigating weakness and internal strength frequently drives us to defy cultural assumptions and standards. Society, on occasion, propagates the legend that strength is inseparable from a shortfall of weakness. The strain to adjust to these beliefs can prompt the concealment of our credible selves, frustrating the improvement of genuine inward strength. Breaking liberated from these assumptions requires a redefinition of solidarity — one that recognizes the mental fortitude it takes to be powerless.

Social impacts likewise assume a huge part in forming how we might interpret weakness and inward strength. In societies that focus on independence and confidence, weakness might be seen as a deviation from the standard. On the other hand, in societies that esteem reliance and aggregate prosperity, weakness might be viewed as a strength, cultivating a feeling of local area and shared help. Exploring the crossing point between social assumptions and individual genuineness turns into an essential part of the excursion towards figuring out weakness and inward strength.

In relational connections, weakness turns into a foundation of closeness and association. At the point when we permit ourselves to be open to other people, we make a space for credibility and profound comprehension. The demonstration of sharing our feelings of dread, dreams, and instabilities cultivates an equal trade, reinforcing the bonds that interface us. Genuine closeness emerges not from flawlessness but rather from the common experience of weakness, where people feel perceived the truth about and acknowledged.

Parental impacts shape the early underpinnings of our relationship with weakness and, accordingly, our inward strength. Kids gain from their guardians about the acknowledgment or dismissal of weakness. Guardians who establish a climate where feelings are recognized and communicated lay the foundation for their youngsters to foster flexibility. By demonstrating sound articulations of weakness, guardians add to the development of inward strength in the future.

The work environment, frequently connected with rivalry and execution, is likewise a space where the elements of weakness and inward strength become possibly the most important factor. Pioneers who show weakness by conceding botches, looking for criticism, and cultivating a culture of open correspondence make a stronger and imaginative workplace. Representatives who have a good sense of reassurance to communicate their thoughts and concerns add to a work environment culture that values realness and coordinated effort.

Investigating weakness and internal strength inside oneself requires a guarantee to mindfulness and self-sympathy. It includes a consistent course of stripping back the layers of self-insurance and facing the uneasiness that goes with genuine realness. This excursion isn't without its difficulties, as cultural molding and previous encounters might have formed our safeguard instruments. Looking for help from specialists, tutors, or care groups can be instrumental in exploring this interior investigation.

Developing self-empathy turns into a fundamental part of the excursion towards figuring out weakness and internal strength. Self-empathy includes treating oneself with generosity and figuring out, particularly in snapshots of weakness. It requires perceiving that being human means being blemished and that embracing weakness is a demonstration of confidence. Through self-empathy, people figure out how to support their internal strength, encouraging a strong mentality that can face life's hardships.

In the domain of imagination, weakness is the impetus for development and creativity. Inventiveness thrives when people will face challenges, rock the boat, and express their remarkable viewpoints. Craftsmen, essayists, and makers draw strength from their weakness, taking advantage of a well of credibility that imbues their work with profundity and reverberation. The innovative strategy itself is an excursion through weakness, an eagerness to investigate the unknown domains of one's creative mind.

Care rehearses, like contemplation and self-reflection, act as important apparatuses in the investigation of weakness and inward strength. These practices develop present-second mindfulness, permitting people to notice their contemplations and feelings without judgment. Care gives an establishment to self-disclosure, revealing the layers of weakness that might be disguised underneath the surface. It offers a pathway to internal strength by encouraging a profound association with the real self.

The connection among weakness and sympathy is advantageous. Sympathy, the capacity to comprehend and discuss the thoughts of another, is elevated when people embrace their own weakness. Through shared human encounters, sympathy turns into a scaffold that interfaces people, encouraging a feeling of understanding and empathy. This interconnectedness adds to the strength of networks and social orders, making a texture woven with the strings of weakness and sympathy.

The recuperating system, whether physical or profound, frequently includes an excursion through weakness. In remedial settings, people stand up to their weaknesses, unwinding the layers of agony and injury. The helpful relationship itself is based on a groundwork of trust, where weakness turns into the course for mending and development. Through the affirmation of weakness, people set out on a way towards versatility and completeness.

The association among weakness and internal strength stretches out past the person to cultural and worldwide settings. Developments for civil rights and uniformity frequently start with people embracing their weakness and sharing their accounts. Promotion for positive change requires an eagerness to defy fundamental treacheries, remaining notwithstanding weakness for everyone's benefit. In these aggregate articulations of weakness, social orders track down the solidarity to destroy harsh designs and construct a more evenhanded future.

2.2 Activities and exercises to help readers embrace and understand their vulnerabilities

Taking part in exercises and activities intended to cultivate mindfulness and comprehension of weaknesses can be an extraordinary excursion towards self-improvement and strengthening. These practices give people the devices to explore the intricacies of their feelings, face fears, and develop a more profound association with their genuine selves. From self-reflection to inventive articulation, the accompanying exercises plan to direct perusers on a way of embracing and grasping their weaknesses.

1. **Journaling:**
   Journaling is a strong and open instrument for self-reflection. Put away devoted time every day to expound on your viewpoints, sentiments, and encounters. Investigate snapshots of weakness, taking note of any examples or repeating subjects. Journaling considers a private and non-critical space to communicate your thoughts, giving experiences into your profound scene and cultivating a more profound comprehension of your weaknesses.

2. **Care Contemplation:**
   Care contemplation is a training that develops present-second mindfulness. By zeroing in on the breath or noticing considerations without connection, people can foster a more prominent comprehension of their feelings. Care permits you to notice weaknesses without judgment, making space for self-sympathy. Integrate care into your everyday practice through directed reflections or care applications, progressively constructing an establishment for a more cognizant and deliberate life.

3. **Body Output Exercise:**
   The body examine is a care practice that includes pointing out various pieces of the body. This exercise energizes familiarity with actual sensations and profound

reactions. Rests or sit easily, and gradually check your body from head to toe. Notice any pressure, distress, or feelings that emerge. Associating with your body in this manner can extend how you might interpret how feelings manifest truly, helping you perceive and embrace weakness.

4. **Representation Strategies:**
Representation activities can help with investigating and figuring out weaknesses. Shut your eyes and envision a protected and quiet spot. Envision yourself here, and steadily present circumstances or feelings that trigger weakness. Notice your responses and feelings in this controlled climate. Representation permits you to defy weaknesses in a delicate way, giving an open door to self-empathy and reflection.

5. **Imaginative Articulation:**
Taking part in imaginative exercises, like drawing, painting, or composing verse, gives a non-verbal outlet to communicating weaknesses. Imaginative articulation takes into consideration the correspondence of mind boggling feelings that might be trying to verbally understandable. Make without judgment, it be restorative to let the actual cycle. The subsequent fine art can act as a visual portrayal of your excursion towards embracing weakness.

6. **Letter Composing:**
Compose a letter to yourself, communicating weaknesses, fears, and expectations. Move toward this letter with self-sympathy, recognizing that weaknesses are a characteristic piece of the human experience. On the other hand, consider composing a letter to somebody you trust, discussing your thoughts and encounters. The demonstration of expressing feelings can be soothing, cultivating a feeling of association with yourself as well as other people.

7. **Appreciation Practice:**
Developing appreciation can move the concentration from weaknesses to qualities and positive parts of life. Consistently record three things you are thankful for. This training empowers an outlook shift, encouraging a feeling of appreciation for both the difficulties and favors in your day to day existence. Appreciation can be a useful asset in rethinking weaknesses as any open doors for development and learning.

8. **Bunch Conversations and Backing Circles:**
Taking part in transparent conversations inside a steady social environment can give approval and a feeling of association. Joining a help circle or partaking in bunch treatment permits people to share their weaknesses, acknowledging they are in good company in their encounters. Undivided attention and compassion inside a social scene can add to an aggregate excursion of understanding and embracing weaknesses.

9. **Pretending Activities:**
Pretending practices permit people to investigate various situations that trigger weaknesses. Enroll the assistance of a confided in companion or specialist to

participate in pretending discussions. This interaction empowers you to work on answering weakness instigating circumstances, engaging you with successful correspondence systems and close to home guideline methods.

10. **Self-Sympathy Contemplation:**

    Self-sympathy reflection includes coordinating sensations of benevolence and understanding towards oneself. Track down a peaceful space, shut your eyes, and rehash confirming expressions, for example, "May I be caring to myself" or "I deserve love and acknowledgment." This training cultivates self-sympathy, neutralizing self-decisive considerations related with weaknesses and supporting a gentler relationship with oneself.

11. **Limit Setting Activities:**

    Understanding and defining individual limits is pivotal in exploring weaknesses. Consider your solace levels and distinguish regions where you might have to lay out limits. Practice decisive correspondence in communicating your requirements and cutoff points. Defining and keeping up with sound limits is an enabling activity that supports an identity regard and security.

12. **Close to home Guideline Methods:**

    Figuring out how to manage feelings is crucial in exploring weaknesses actually. Investigate strategies like profound breathing, moderate muscle unwinding, or directed symbolism. These practices help in overseeing extreme feelings, considering a more adjusted and careful reaction to weakness prompting circumstances.

13. **Job of Humor:**

    Humor can be a significant device in easing up the profound load of weaknesses. Track down humor in your encounters, and make it a point to chuckle at yourself. Share happy minutes with others, making an air that permits weaknesses to be drawn closer with a feeling of flexibility and bliss.

14. **Perusing and Instruction:**

    Extend how you might interpret weakness through writing, brain science books, and exploration regarding the matter. Acquire experiences from specialists, for example, Brene Brown, who investigates weakness and its extraordinary power. Teaching yourself on the mental parts of weakness upgrades mindfulness and gives a structure to exploring and embracing weaknesses.

15. **Nature Association:**

    Investing energy in nature can give a feeling of comfort and association. Go for a stroll in a recreation area, sit by a stream, or invest energy in a characteristic setting. Nature has an establishing impact and can act as a background for reflection. Utilize this opportunity to think about weaknesses, perceiving the interconnectedness of the regular world and your own excursion.

16. **Insistence Practice:**

    Integrate positive insistences into your day to day daily schedule. Make certifications that neutralize negative self-talk related with weaknesses. Rehash these insistences routinely, building up a positive and engaging story about yourself. Insistences add to building a strong outlook and developing self-sympathy.

17. **Humanitarian effort:**
Taking part in volunteer exercises furnishes a chance to associate with others and gain viewpoint on shared human encounters. Chipping in can make a feeling of direction and add to a more extensive comprehension of weaknesses inside the setting of a local area. Thoughtful gestures and administration can likewise be a wellspring of individual strengthening.

18. **Close to home Registrations:**
Consistently check in with your feelings to foster an uplifted consciousness of your psychological and close to home states. Make a day to day or week after week schedule for close to home registrations, noticing any examples or triggers related with weaknesses. This training upgrades the capacity to understand individuals on a profound level and encourages a proactive way to deal with taking care of oneself.

19. **Positive Perception:**
Envision positive results when confronted with weaknesses. Envision yourself exploring testing circumstances with flexibility and beauty. Positive representation can impact your outlook, imparting a feeling of certainty and strength despite weaknesses.

20. **Intelligent Perusing and Composing:**

Investigate writing, sonnets, or statements that reverberate with the subject of weakness. Peruse and think about the expressions of creators who have shared their weaknesses transparently. Utilize intelligent composition to offer your viewpoints and responses to these readings, interfacing with the common human experience of weakness.

2.3 Real-life examples of individuals who turned vulnerability into a source of strength

Genuine instances of people who have changed weakness into a wellspring of solidarity give strong stories of flexibility, mental fortitude, and legitimacy. These accounts represent that embracing weakness is definitely not an indication of shortcoming yet a pathway to self-improvement and strengthening. From well known people to regular legends, these people have exhibited the extraordinary force of weakness in different parts of their lives.

One convincing model is the narrative of Oprah Winfrey, a news magnate, giver, and persuasive character. All through her vocation, Oprah has transparently shared her own battles, including a troublesome youth set apart by destitution and misuse.

By helplessly describing her encounters on her syndicated program, she associated with a great many watchers as well as broken the shame encompassing subjects like maltreatment and injury. Oprah's credibility and eagerness to be powerless have added to her monstrous effect, transforming her own excursion into a wellspring of solidarity for her and others.

Brene Brown, an exploration teacher and creator, has turned into a main voice on weakness and boldness. In her TED Talk and resulting books, Earthy colored shares her exploration discoveries on weakness, disgrace, and compassion. Her work has reverberated worldwide, motivating innumerable people to embrace weakness as a wellspring of solidarity. Earthy colored's receptiveness about her battles and her obligation to destigmatizing weakness have started a development that urges individuals to make an appearance truly in their lives.

In the realm of sports, Michael Phelps, the most embellished Olympian ever, has been authentic about his psychological wellness challenges. In spite of his striking progress in swimming, Phelps confronted subtle conflicts, including nervousness and melancholy. By sharing his weaknesses, Phelps has turned into a supporter for emotional wellness mindfulness, stressing that looking for help is an indication of solidarity. His transparency has destigmatized emotional well-being issues as well as motivated others to focus on their prosperity.

Malala Yousafzai, a Nobel laureate and supporter for young ladies' schooling, epitomizes transforming weakness into strength even with misfortune. Malala endure a Taliban death endeavor for her frank promotion. Rather than capitulating to fear, she proceeded with her battle for training privileges, even after the horrible occurrence. Malala's strength and resolute obligation to her goal grandstand how weakness, when defied with boldness, can fuel a strong development for change.

Another powerful model is J.K. Rowling, the creator of the gigantically famous Harry Potter series. Prior to her prosperity, Rowling confronted various individual difficulties, including neediness and the deficiency of her mom. At the point when she composed the primary book, she was a striving single parent managing despondency. Rowling's weakness is clear in her open conversations about psychological well-being and the close to home battles she confronted. In spite of the underlying dismissal of her composition, Rowling continued, transforming weakness into the groundwork of her abstract inheritance.

The music business has seen craftsmen who channel weakness into their inventive articulation. Adele, known for her deep and genuinely charged music, has been straightforward about the individual heartbreaks that roused her melodies. By uncovering her inner self through her verses, Adele has made a profound association with her crowd. Her weakness has turned into the wellspring of her imaginative strength, reverberating with audience members around the world.

In the domain of activism, Greta Thunberg, a youthful environmental change extremist, has valiantly voiced her interests about the natural emergency. Thunberg's weakness is apparent in her profound discourses, where she communicates disappointment and earnestness about the condition of the planet. As opposed to avoiding her feelings, Thunberg involves her weakness to prepare a worldwide development for environment activity, demonstrating that credibility can be an impetus for change.

On a more private level, think about the tale of Maya, an overcomer of aggressive behavior at home. Maya's weakness was tied in with getting away from an oppressive relationship as well as about ending the quiet encompassing abusive behavior at home. By sharing her story, Maya enabled herself as well as other people to look for help and break the pattern of misuse. Her weakness turned into the wellspring of solidarity that prompted mending and backing inside her local area.

In the business world, business visionaries like Sara Blakely, the organizer behind Spanx, have embraced weakness as a feature of their authority process. Blakely straightforwardly examines her disappointments and dismissals prior to making progress. Her eagerness to share the weakness innate in business has enlivened hopeful business pioneers to explore difficulties with versatility and steadiness.

These genuine models highlight that weakness is a general encounter that rises above contrasts in foundation, achievement, or distinction. Every story features the extraordinary capability of embracing weakness and transforming it into a wellspring of solidarity. Whether it's through sharing individual battles, pushing for social change, or making workmanship, these people have shown the way that genuineness and boldness can rise up out of weakness.

These models likewise challenge cultural discernments that weakness is an indication of shortcoming. All things being equal, they reclassify weakness as a bold demonstration that includes confronting one's reality, offering it to other people, and involving it as an impetus for development. The people referenced above have changed their own lives as well as significantly affected the existences of others by normalizing weakness and empowering open discussions about difficulties and wins.

Additionally, the models feature the far reaching influence of weakness. At the point when people share their true stories, they make a cascading type of influence, moving others to do likewise. This interconnected trap of weakness encourages a feeling of local area and backing, it is disconnecting to expose the fantasy that weakness. It turns into a shared encounter that reinforces bonds, energizes compassion, and advances aggregate recuperating.

Basically, these genuine models insist that weakness is certainly not a static state however a unique power that can be saddled for individual and aggregate strengthening. The excursion from weakness to strength includes self-reflection, flexibility, and an eagerness to face distress.

It requires a change in context that sees weakness not as an impediment but rather as a wellspring of validness and potential.

As people think about these accounts, they might track down motivation to set out on their own excursion of embracing weakness. Whether in private connections, imaginative pursuits, or backing, the illustrations from these models urge people to make an appearance really, recognize their weaknesses, and perceive the innate strength that rises up out of such genuineness.

All in all, genuine instances of people who have transformed weakness into a wellspring of solidarity act as reference points of motivation and versatility. From worldwide figures to regular legends, these accounts exhibit the extraordinary force of embracing weakness. They challenge cultural standards, separate marks of shame, and make an aggregate story that reclassifies weakness as a gallant and engaging power. As these people share their legitimate encounters, they welcome others to do likewise, cultivating a culture of transparency, association, and aggregate strength.

Embracing weakness and changing it into a wellspring of solidarity is a significant excursion that addresses the actual center of the human experience. A cycle requires a change in context, testing the ordinary thought that weakness is an indication of short-coming. All things being equal, it welcomes people to perceive the inborn power and mental fortitude that can emerge from being open, legitimate, and able to confront the vulnerabilities of life.

One praiseworthy person who encapsulates the change of weakness into strength is Brené Brown, an examination teacher, and creator. Earthy colored's work, especially her investigation of weakness and disgrace, has resounded all around the world, start-ing discussions and motivating endless people to embrace their weaknesses. In her TED Talk and resulting books, Brown underlines that weakness isn't an obligation yet the origination of development, imagination, and veritable association.

Brown's own excursion of understanding weakness started through her examina-tion on disgrace flexibility. She found that the people who were versatile even with disgrace had a typical quality - the eagerness to be defenseless. In her book "Trying Significantly," Brown presents the idea of "sincere living," which includes embracing weakness, developing self-empathy, and relinquishing the legend of flawlessness.

One vital part of Earthy colored's work is the qualification between fitting in and having a place. Fitting in, she contends, is tied in with trim oneself to measure up to outside assumptions, while having a place is tied in with being acknowledged for who we really are. Embracing weakness is the pathway to genuine having a place, as it requires showing up truly, in any event, when it implies taking a chance with dismissal or judgment.

In the domain of emotional well-being backing, endless people have transformed their own battles into wellsprings of solidarity. Consider the tale of Kevin Hines, who endure a self destruction endeavor by leaping off the Brilliant Door Extension. Hines straightforwardly shares his fight with bipolar turmoil and the dull minutes that drove him to that critical day. Presently, he has turned into a strong supporter for psycho-logical wellness mindfulness, talking internationally about the significance of breaking the shame encompassing emotional well-being.

Hines' weakness about his psychological well-being difficulties has not exclusively been groundbreaking for him by and by yet has additionally saved lives by empower-ing others to look for help. His story represents the capability of weakness to interface, motivate, and make positive change.

In the imaginative expressions, weakness is much of the time the main impetus behind strong and suggestive works. Consider the music of vocalist lyricist Demi Lovato, who has been straightforward about her battles with emotional well-being, enslavement, and self-perception. Lovato's tunes, for example, "High rise" and "Sober," dig into her weaknesses with crude genuineness.

By sharing her excursion through music, Lovato has made a space for audience members to connect with their own battles. Her weakness has turned into a wellspring of solidarity for herself as well as for the people who track down comfort and grasping in her specialty. Lovato's transparency is a demonstration of the groundbreaking force of embracing weakness inside the inventive strategy.

In the domain of activism, Malala Yousafzai stands apart as a person who transformed weakness into an impetus for worldwide change. Malala confronted outrageous risk and difficulty as a little kid supporting for training in Pakistan. She endure a Taliban death endeavor and, as opposed to withdrawing in dread, proceeded with her support with much more prominent assurance.

Malala's weakness notwithstanding viciousness changed her into an image of flexibility and mental fortitude. She stands up for young ladies' schooling as well as fills in as a living illustration of how one's weaknesses can be bridled to light a worldwide development for equity and equity.

On an additional individual level, ordinary legends exhibit the extraordinary force of weakness. Consider the narrative of Alex, an overcomer of aggressive behavior at home, who tracked down the solidarity to leave a harmful relationship and offer her experience. By talking transparently about the difficulties she confronted and the most common way of modifying her life, Alex has turned into a backer for others confronting comparative circumstances.

Her weakness fills in as an encouraging sign, demonstrating the way that strength can rise out of the most obscure minutes. Alex's story represents the effect of individual weakness on making a steady local area and moving others to look for help.

In the corporate world, pioneers who embrace weakness can encourage conditions that focus on genuineness and advancement. The late Steve Occupations, prime supporter of Macintosh Inc., was known for his capacity to straightforwardly recognize disappointments and misfortunes. Occupations' weakness was obvious when he got back to Apple in the wake of being removed from the organization he helped to establish.

In his beginning location at Stanford College, Occupations shared individual tales of accomplishment and disappointment, accentuating the significance of following one's instinct and embracing life's difficulties. His readiness to be weak about his own process has roused incalculable business people and business pioneers to move toward misfortunes with flexibility and a development outlook.

In the field of sports, Michael Phelps, the most embellished Olympian ever, has been open about his battles with psychological wellness, including tension and misery. Notwithstanding his uncommon outcome in the pool, Phelps confronted inside fights that drove him to mull over self destruction. By transparently examining his weaknesses, Phelps has turned into a supporter for emotional well-being mindfulness, underlining that looking for help is an indication of solidarity.

Phelps' weakness has not just broken the shame around psychological wellness in sports yet has likewise energized competitors and people from varying backgrounds to focus on their psychological prosperity. His process represents that weakness isn't restricted to explicit spaces however is a widespread part of the human experience.

In the realm of writing, J.K. Rowling, the creator of the Harry Potter series, has shared her encounters of destitution, misery, and the difficulties of being a single parent prior to making progress. Rowling's weakness is apparent in her ability to talk straightforwardly about her battles, in any event, during times when she confronted dismissal from distributers.

Her excursion from weakness to progress resounds with hopeful scholars and people confronting affliction. Rowling's story highlights that embracing weakness isn't just about uncovering one's battles yet additionally about continuing on through them and involving them as venturing stones to more noteworthy accomplishments.

Besides, weakness assumes a vital part in relational connections, as found in the narrative of David and Julie. This couple confronted the test of exploring through a surprising wellbeing emergency when Julie was determined to have a constant sickness. Rather than concealing their feelings of trepidation and vulnerabilities, they decided to be open to one another.

By transparently conveying their feelings and concerns, David and Julie reinforced their bond and made an underpinning of trust. Their weakness permitted them to confront the difficulties together, supporting that transparency in connections can cultivate versatility and extend associations.

In the domain of personal development, people frequently transform weakness into strength through purposeful practices. Take the case of Maria, who battled with self-uncertainty and an inability to embrace success in her expert life. Perceiving the requirement for change, Maria looked for treatment to investigate the underlying foundations of her weaknesses and work towards self-strengthening.

Through self-reflection and weakness, Maria defeated her inability to embrace success as well as found newly discovered certainty. Her deliberate obligation to personal growth features how weakness can be an impetus for self-improvement and self-revelation.

These different models aggregately highlight the all inclusive nature of weakness and its extraordinary likely across different parts of life. From the public spotlight to the close spaces of individual connections, weakness arises as a power that, when saddled with boldness, can prompt significant strength and flexibility.

What brings together these accounts is the acknowledgment that weakness is definitely not a one-time occasion however a continuous course of self-revelation and genuineness. It includes recognizing defects, confronting fears, and being available to the vulnerabilities of life. The people referenced above didn't keep away from weakness; all things being equal, they inclined toward it, involving their encounters as fuel for individual and aggregate development.

The extraordinary excursion from weakness to strength frequently includes a few key components:

Mindfulness: Embracing weakness starts with mindfulness — recognizing one's contemplations, feelings, and difficulties. This contemplative cycle permits people to comprehend the wellsprings of weakness and the effect it has on their lives.

Valiant Articulation: Transforming weakness into strength requires the fortitude to communicate one's legitimate self. This might include sharing individual stories, conceding botches, or facing troublesome feelings. Genuine articulation cultivates association and assembles scaffolds of understanding with others.

Local area and Association: Weakness flourishes within the sight of a steady local area. Sharing weaknesses inside a believed circle makes a feeling of having a place and lessens sensations of seclusion. The force of aggregate encounters fortifies people and networks the same.

Learning and Development Mentality: Embracing weakness includes taking on a development outlook — a conviction that difficulties are potential open doors for learning and development. People who see weakness as a venturing stone to self-improvement are bound to explore challenges with versatility.

Reflection and Combination: The groundbreaking system requires reflection on previous encounters and a promise to incorporating examples learned. It includes embracing weakness not as a previous occasion but rather as a continuous part of life that adds to progressing self-improvement.

As people explore this groundbreaking excursion, they might experience obstruction from cultural assumptions, incorporated convictions, or fears of judgment. The models referenced before exhibit that the awards of embracing weakness — credible associations, self-awareness, and positive effect — far offset the difficulties.

Basically, weakness turns into a wellspring of solidarity when people pick genuineness over similarity, flexibility over evasion, and association over confinement. A unique power welcomes people to step into the field of their lives, as Brené Brown expressively puts it, and to dare enormously notwithstanding the vulnerabilities.

Chapter 3

The Power of Self-Reflection

In the rushing about of our regular routines, the idea of self-reflection frequently assumes a lower priority. We wind up trapped in a hurricane of exercises, attempting to beat the clock to fulfill time constraints, satisfy liabilities, and explore the intricacies of current presence. In the midst of this mayhem, the force of self-reflection is an underutilized apparatus that holds the possibility to change our lives.

Self-reflection is definitely not a simple contemplative activity; it is a significant excursion into the profundities of our viewpoints, feelings, and activities. It is a purposeful and cognizant work to stop, step back, and look at the embroidery of our lives. This cycle requires a readiness to stand up to both the light and shadow parts of our being, stripping away the layers of molding and cultural assumptions to uncover the bona fide self underneath.

The excited speed of contemporary life frequently beats thoughtfulness down. The requests of work, family, and social commitments can leave us feeling like ceaseless performers, offsetting different obligations with brief period for self-disclosure. However, in the midst of this bedlam, lies the dumbfounding truth: the more tumultuous life turns into, the more essential self-reflection becomes for keeping up with equilibrium and prosperity.

The excursion of self-reflection starts with cutting out purposeful snapshots of isolation. In the quietude of these minutes, we can disconnect ourselves from the outer commotion and turn our consideration internal. It is here of tranquility that the murmurs of our deepest contemplations become discernible, directing us to investigate the maze of our own personalities.

As we set out on this reflective journey, moving toward it with an open heart and a non-critical mindset is fundamental. Self-reflection isn't about self-judgment or culpability; rather, it is a merciful assessment of our decisions and ways of behaving. By developing self-empathy, we establish a safe and sustaining climate that permits us to investigate the openings of our mind unafraid of cruel self-judgment.

One of the vital advantages of self-reflection is the increased mindfulness it brings. As we dive into our viewpoints and feelings, we gain experiences into the fundamental inspirations that drive our activities. This mindfulness fills in as an incredible asset for self-improvement, empowering us to settle on informed choices lined up with our qualities and desires.

Besides, self-reflection cultivates a more profound comprehension of our associations with others. By analyzing our relational elements, we can recognize examples of correspondence, areas of contention, and open doors for association. This freshly discovered mindfulness engages us to develop better and additional satisfying connections, encouraging compassion and common comprehension.

In the domain of self-awareness, the force of self-reflection lies in its capacity to uncover restricting convictions and deliberate obstructions. A considerable lot of us convey stuff from an earlier time — view of insufficiency, anxiety toward disappointment, or a hesitance to get out of our usual ranges of familiarity. Through self-reflection, we can go up against these obstructions head-on, destroying the psychological builds that prevent our development.

The groundbreaking capability of self-reflection reaches out to the domain of the capacity to understand anyone on a profound level. By leveling up our skill to perceive and comprehend our feelings, we improve our ability for self-guideline. This, thus, empowers us to explore life's difficulties with more prominent strength and self-restraint, encouraging profound prosperity.

Moreover, self-reflection fills in as a compass for adjusting our activities to our fundamental beliefs. In the whirlwind of outer tensions and cultural assumptions, it is not difficult to neglect to focus on the main thing to us. Standard self-reflection goes about as a recalibration component, directing us back to our credible selves and provoking us to live as one with our most profound feelings.

The force of self-reflection isn't restricted to snapshots of isolation; it stretches out to our capacity to gain from life's encounters. Each achievement, disappointment, happiness, and distress offers a rich embroidery of examples ready to be unwound. Through self-reflection, we can separate significance from our encounters, refining intelligence that pushes us forward on our life process.

Chasing self-reflection, journaling arises as an important sidekick. The demonstration of putting pen to paper fills in as a substantial articulation of our deepest contemplations and sentiments. Journaling gives a material on which we can lay out the scene of our brains, taking into consideration a more far reaching investigation of our inward world.

Be that as it may, the force of self-reflection isn't exclusively a singular undertaking. It stretches out to the shared perspective, affecting the manner in which we draw in with the world and add to the more noteworthy entirety. As people become more receptive to their internal identities, an expanding influence follows, encouraging a culture of sympathy, credibility, and understanding.

In the work environment, the advantages of self-reflection manifest in upgraded authority and group elements. Pioneers who take part in ordinary reflection are better outfitted to lead with credibility and rouse everyone around them. Colleagues, thus, benefit from a cooperative climate where open correspondence and common regard win.

Besides, the force of self-reflection is clear in its job in compromise. At the point when people carve out opportunity to ponder their own viewpoints and predispositions, they are bound to move toward clashes with a receptive outlook. This ability to comprehend assorted perspectives establishes the groundwork for productive discourse and goal.

In the instructive circle, the combination of self-reflection encourages an affection for deep rooted learning. Understudies who are urged to consider their growth opportunities foster metacognitive abilities — the capacity to contemplate and direct their own reasoning cycles. This metacognitive mindfulness improves scholarly execution as well as plans understudies for the intricate difficulties representing things to come.

On a cultural level, the force of self-reflection is an impetus for social change. At the point when people on the whole participate in contemplation, they become more receptive to the foundational issues that pervade society. This increased mindfulness lays the preparation for support, activism, and an aggregate obligation to encouraging an additional fair and impartial world.

The excursion of self-reflection isn't without its difficulties. It expects mental fortitude to stand up to the parts of ourselves that we might see as awkward or new. However, in this distress genuine development and change live. The force of self-reflection lies in its ability to lead us past the outer layer of our characters, welcoming us to investigate the profundities of our realness.

As we explore the maze of self-revelation, embracing the recurring pattern of the process is fundamental. Self-reflection is definitely not a straight excursion with a foreordained objective; rather, it is a consistent pattern of investigation, disclosure, and development. Every snapshot of reflection strips away another layer, uncovering new features of our character and welcoming us to embrace the consistently unfurling secret of self.

In the domain of otherworldliness, self-reflection is a consecrated practice that rises above the limits of oneself. It is an excursion into the interconnectedness, everything being equal, an acknowledgment of the unity that underlies variety. Through self-reflection, people tap into a wellspring of intelligence that reaches out past private information — an all inclusive cognizance that joins together and supports all of presence.

The force of self-reflection isn't a panacea for the difficulties of life, nor is it a one-size-fits-all arrangement. A dynamic and diverse device adjusts to the special shapes of every individual's excursion. Some might track down comfort in reflection, others in creative articulation, regardless, others in significant discussions with confided in associates.

Chasing self-reflection, developing a feeling of interest and wonder is significant. Move toward every snapshot of thoughtfulness with the transparency of a fledgling's brain, liberated from assumptions or assumptions. Here of interest, the customary changes into the exceptional, and the ordinary turns into a material for significant self-revelation.

The force of self-reflection isn't bound to explicit minutes or customs; it penetrates the texture of our regular routines. It is available in the delay between breaths, the tranquility before activity, and the peaceful snapshots of thought before rest. As we imbue self-reflection into the embroidery of our reality, it turns into a directing power that shapes our discernments, decisions, and eventually, our fates.

However, in the midst of the clatter of day to day existence, the call to self-reflect is in many cases overwhelmed by the commotion of outside interruptions. The ceaseless requests of innovation, the charm of moment delight, and the tensions of cultural assumptions make a racket that suffocates the delicate murmurs of our internal identities. In this time of consistent network, the force of self-reflection turns into an offset — a safe-haven of tranquility amidst a turbulent world.

3.1 Techniques for self-reflection and introspection

In the domain of self-improvement and self-revelation, strategies for self-reflection and contemplation act as important apparatuses to explore the maze of one's viewpoints, feelings, and encounters. These methods give an organized way to deal with thoughtfulness, empowering people to acquire further bits of knowledge into themselves and develop an increased identity mindfulness. As we investigate different strategies for self-reflection, it's fundamental to perceive that the viability of these procedures can change from one individual to another. The vital lies in finding the methodology or mix of approaches that resound most legitimately with every person.

One generally polished strategy for self-reflection is journaling. The demonstration of putting pen to paper makes a substantial record of one's viewpoints, sentiments, and encounters. An intelligent diary fills in as a confidential space to investigate the inward scene, offering a safe-haven for unfiltered self-articulation. Whether as everyday reflections, appreciation records, or continuous flow composing, journaling gives a chance to follow designs, recognize sets off, and reveal the hidden inspirations that deeply influence conduct.

One more impressive strategy for self-reflection is care contemplation. Established in old pondering practices, care includes developing a non-critical familiarity with the current second. Through practices, for example, centered breathing, body examine reflection, or careful perception, people foster the ability to notice their contemplations and feelings without connection. This elevated mindfulness encourages a profound comprehension of oneself, permitting people to observe the recurring pattern of their inward encounters.

Directed representation is a method that outfits the force of creative mind for self-reflection. By making mental pictures that address different parts of one's life, people can investigate wants, fears, and yearnings. Directed perception practices frequently include imagining an optimal future, picturing outcome in a specific undertaking, or in any event, returning to previous encounters to acquire new experiences. This procedure takes advantage of the innovative resources of the psyche, giving an extraordinary focal point through which people can investigate their inward scenes.

Self-addressing is an immediate and reflective method that includes offering intriguing conversation starters to oneself. These inquiries brief people to dive into their convictions, values, and yearnings. Instances of self-intelligent inquiries incorporate "What gives me pleasure?" "What are my basic beliefs?" and "What steps might I at any point take to adjust my activities to my qualities?" By participating in a deliberate request, people can unwind layers of self-discernment and gain lucidity on their valid selves.

Creative articulation, like composition, drawing, or painting, can be a strong mode for self-reflection. The innovative flow fills in as a channel for subliminal considerations and feelings to surface. Creative undertakings offer a non-direct and non-verbal method for self-articulation, permitting people to get to and convey parts of their inward universes that might be trying to verbally understandable. The subsequent manifestations can act as mirrors mirroring the deepest considerations and sensations of the maker.

Taking part in transparent discussions with believed friends is a social way to deal with self-reflection. Imparting one's contemplations and encounters to others gives a new point of view as well as cultivates a feeling of association and backing. The demonstration of expressing considerations can carry lucidity to complex feelings and welcome bits of knowledge from the people who offer an alternate vantage point. Significant discussions make a common space for shared thoughtfulness, building up the possibility that self-reflection isn't exclusively a singular undertaking yet can be enhanced through public investigation.

Careful development rehearses, like yoga or kendo, incorporate actual work with deliberate mindfulness. These practices accentuate the psyche body association, empowering people to be completely present in every development.

The cadenced progression of careful development fills in as a moving reflection, welcoming people to notice their sensations, contemplations, and breath. By integrating care into actual work, people can encourage a comprehensive way to deal with mindfulness.

The act of self-reflection can be improved using intelligent prompts. These prompts, whether as composed questions, statements, or confirmations, give an organized structure to consideration. For instance, people might pick an everyday reflection brief to contemplate over the course of the day, directing their considerations toward explicit parts of their lives. Intelligent prompts go about as delicate pokes, focusing on areas of self-awareness and investigation.

Quiet withdraws offer a more vivid and escalated climate for self-reflection. Whether as reflection withdraws, nature withdraws, or computerized detox withdraws, these encounters give a brief reprieve from the interruptions of regular daily existence. In the casing of quietness and isolation, people have the space to participate in profound thoughtfulness, liberated from the outer upgrades that frequently cloud mindfulness. Quiet withdraws set out a freedom for people to pay attention to the murmurs of their internal identities without the clamor of the rest of the world.

Dream examination is a method that takes advantage of the psyche brain's representative language. Keeping a fantasy diary and considering repeating subjects, images, or feelings in dreams can disclose stowed away parts of the mind. Dreams frequently act as a mirror reflecting natural feelings, unsettled clashes, or neglected wants. By unraveling the language of dreams, people can acquire bits of knowledge into their oblivious contemplations and utilize this data for self-awareness.

The act of appreciation is an extraordinary way to deal with self-reflection that spotlights on developing appreciation for the current second. Keeping an appreciation diary, where people consistently list things they are thankful for, shifts the concentration from what might be missing to what is bountiful in one's life. This straightforward yet significant method cultivates a positive mentality and urges people to perceive the magnificence in ordinary encounters. Appreciation turns into a focal point through which people can reexamine their viewpoints and improve their general prosperity.

Nature submersion is a comprehensive procedure that use the helpful advantages of investing energy in regular habitats. Whether through climbing, setting up camp, or essentially walking around a recreation area, interfacing with nature gives a scenery to thought. The sights, sounds, and rhythms of the regular world establish a helpful climate for self-reflection. Nature fills in as a mirror mirroring the recurrent examples of life, empowering people to line up with their own inborn rhythms.

The utilization of innovation for self-reflection has become progressively predominant in the advanced age. Versatile applications, online stages, and virtual networks offer directed activities, prompts, and assets for people trying to participate in self-reflection. These advanced apparatuses give openness and comfort, permitting people to integrate self-reflection into their day to day schedules fully backed by innovation.

It's essential to take note of that the viability of these strategies is affected by individual inclinations, character types, and life conditions. A few people might resound more with pensive practices like contemplation, while others might find expressive outlets like workmanship or development more helpful for self-reflection. Furthermore, the coordination of different methods can make a comprehensive and customized way to deal with self-revelation.

All in all, procedures for self-reflection and contemplation are different and versatile, offering a heap of roads for people to investigate the profundities of their internal universes. The excursion of self-disclosure is a dynamic and developing cycle, and every procedure fills in as a remarkable feature in the mosaic of self-awareness. Whether through journaling, care, inventive articulation, or social investigation, the deliberate act of self-reflection reveals the layers of realness, encouraging a significant association with oneself and the consistently unfurling embroidery of life.

3.2 Journaling prompts and exercises to facilitate self-discovery

Journaling is a strong and open device for self-disclosure, giving a space to thoughtfulness, reflection, and the investigation of one's internal scene. The demonstration of putting pen to paper permits people to dig into their viewpoints, feelings, and encounters, encouraging a more profound comprehension of themselves. To boost the advantages of journaling, integrating prompts and activities can direct the cycle and work with self-revelation on a more significant level.

Morning Pages:

Start your day with a continuous flow composing exercise known as "Morning Pages." Put away a devoted time every morning to compose three pages of unfiltered considerations. This training helps clear mental mess, uncovers repeating designs, and gives experiences into subliminal considerations.

Appreciation Journaling:

Develop a positive outlook by keeping an appreciation diary. Every day, write down three things you're grateful for. This straightforward practice shifts center toward positive parts of life, cultivating a feeling of appreciation and care.

Course of events Reflection:

Make a timetable of your life, stamping critical occasions, accomplishments, and difficulties. Think about how these minutes have formed you. This visual portrayal offers an exhaustive perspective on your life's story and distinguishes examples of development and flexibility.

Letter to Your More youthful Self:

Compose a caring letter to your more youthful self, offering direction, backing, and bits of knowledge acquired through experience. This exercise empowers self-sympathy and gives a viewpoint on self-improvement and versatility.

Values Explanation:

Consider your guiding principle by posting and focusing on them. Consider the reason why each worth is essential to you and how you epitomize these standards in your regular routine. Adjusting your activities to your qualities improves a feeling of direction and realness.

Dream Journaling:

Keep a fantasy diary by recording your fantasies after waking. Investigate the imagery and feelings inside your fantasies, as they frequently offer a window into your psyche mind. Examining repeating subjects might uncover unsettled considerations or wants.

Shadow Work:

Dig into the shadow parts of yourself by journaling about qualities or feelings you view as trying. Recognize and investigate these angles without judgment, understanding that they are basic pieces of your entire self. Shadow work advances self-acknowledgment and combination.

Future Self Journaling:

Imagine your optimal future self in clear detail. Portray the individual you try to turn into, your achievements, and the qualities you exemplify. This exercise explains long haul objectives and gives inspiration to self-improvement.

Choice Diary:

Record critical choices in a choice diary. Consider the elements impacting every choice, the feelings in question, and the results. Dissecting past choices upgrades thinking abilities and encourages mindfulness.

Self-Representation:

Draw or compose a nitty gritty depiction of yourself, both truly and inwardly. Investigate how you see your personality and how it lines up with your valid self. This inventive activity supports a more profound association with mental self view.

Close to home Registration:

Consistently check in with your feelings by depicting how you feel at the time. Distinguish the particular feelings and their power. This training upgrades the ability to understand anyone on a deeper level and advances self-guideline.

List of must-dos Journaling:

Make a list of must-dos of encounters, objectives, and yearnings. Consider the reason why every thing is influential for you and how seeking after these desires lines up with your qualities. This exercise supports a feeling of direction and experience.

Care Journaling:

Practice care by portraying your tactile encounters exhaustively. Notice sights, sounds, scents, tastes, and surfaces in your current circumstance. This type of present-second mindfulness advances establishing and a profound association with the present time and place.

Thinking about Difficulties:

Diary about challenges you've confronted, investigating the examples learned and qualities acquired. Pondering difficulty cultivates versatility and gives a guide to exploring future troubles.

Five-Year Projection:

Project yourself five years into the future and depict your life exhaustively. Think about private, proficient, and social viewpoints. This exercise explains long haul objectives and persuades purposeful activity in the present.

Character Representations:

Make character portrayals of huge individuals in your day to day existence. Consider the characteristics you respect, appreciate, or track down testing in every individual. This exercise extends how you might interpret relational elements.

Mind-Guide Investigation:

Use mind-planning methods to investigate interconnected considerations and thoughts outwardly. This nonlinear methodology permits you to uncover relationship between different parts of your life, starting imagination and uncovering stowed away associations.

Pondering Accomplishments:

Recognize and praise your accomplishments, both of all shapes and sizes. Expound on the abilities, endeavors, and determination that added to your prosperity. Considering achievements cultivates a positive mental self portrait and lifts confidence.

Addressing Suspicions:

Challenge your suspicions and convictions by scrutinizing their starting points and legitimacy. Distinguish convictions that might restrict your true capacity or add to self-question. This exercise energizes a change in context and the investigation of elective perspectives.

Everyday Reflection:

Put away opportunity each night for a short reflection on your day. Expound on eminent occasions, feelings, and cooperations. This everyday practice advances mindfulness and a nonstop association with your developing story.

Relationship Elements:

Diary about your connections, investigating elements, correspondence designs, and close to home associations. Consider how every relationship adds to your development and prosperity. This exercise improves social mindfulness.

Similarities and Representations:

Offer your viewpoints and sentiments through similarities or representations. Contrast parts of your existence with items, components, or situations. This innovative methodology gives new bits of knowledge into your encounters.

Individual Mantras:

Foster individual mantras or attestations that resound with your qualities and yearnings. Think of them in your diary routinely, building up sure self-talk and developing a mentality lined up with your objectives.

Body Output Journaling:

Practice a body filter contemplation and diary about the sensations you see in each piece of your body. This care practice improves physical mindfulness and energizes a more profound psyche body association.

Persuasive Statements Reflection:

Select a significant statement and ponder its pertinence to your life. Investigate how the insight epitomized in the statement can direct your activities and mentality. This exercise draws motivation from outer sources to improve self-reflection.

Future Letter to Yourself:

Compose a letter to your future self, communicating expectations, desires, and exhortation. Seal the letter and put it down on the calendar in the future to open it. This exercise makes a fleeting scaffold, permitting you to observe your development over the long haul.

Media Impact Journaling:

Think about the impact of media, including virtual entertainment, on your viewpoints and feelings. Consider how openness to various types of media shapes your discernments and values. This exercise energizes media education and mindfulness.

Unsent Letters:

Compose unsent letters to people who have affected your life, whether emphatically or adversely. Offer your viewpoints and feelings truly, without the goal of sending the letters. This helpful activity takes into account profound delivery and conclusion.

Occasional Reflections:

Think about the changing seasons and their imagery in your life. Think about the equals between regular cycles and your self-awareness. This exercise empowers a familiarity with the repeating idea of life.

Representation Journaling:

Take part in directed perception activities and diary about the pictures, sentiments, and bits of knowledge that emerge. Representation upgrades inventive reasoning and gives a special pathway to investigate your psyche mind.

Future Heritage:

Consider the heritage you wish to abandon. Consider the effect you need to have on others and the world. This forward-looking activity supports deliberate living and adjusting present activities to a significant inheritance.

Interest Journaling:

Move toward your journaling practice with a feeling of interest. Investigate unassuming inquiries and obscure parts of yourself. Develop a demeanor of interest toward your viewpoints, feelings, and encounters.

Individual Stock:

Direct a far reaching individual stock by posting your assets, shortcomings, values, and abilities. Consider how this mindfulness can illuminate your own and proficient turn of events.

Space for Unanswered Inquiries:

Commit a segment of your diary to unanswered inquiries and vulnerabilities. Embrace the distress of uncertainty and permit space for continuous investigation. This training develops persistence and a capacity to bear uncertainty.

Time Case Passage:

Compose a period case passage, catching your ongoing considerations, feelings, and yearnings. Seal the section and return to it sometime in the future. This intelligent activity gives a depiction of your current self for future reflection.

3.3 How self-reflection contributes to building inner strength

Self-reflection, a purposeful and cognizant course of looking at one's viewpoints, feelings, and activities, fills in as a foundation in the development of inward strength. This significant excursion into the openings of one's being gives a ripe ground to self-improvement, flexibility, and an extended comprehension of oneself. As people take part in the act of self-reflection, they uncover the devices and bits of knowledge important to strengthen their inward centers, cultivating a powerful establishment that can face life's hardships.

At its pith, self-reflection is a journey of mindfulness. It is the cognizant investigation of one's own brain, a deliberate interruption in the midst of the noise of day to day existence to unwind the complexities of one's viewpoints and feelings. This elevated mindfulness turns into the bedrock whereupon inward strength is assembled. Understanding the subtleties of one's internal world establishes the groundwork for informed direction, profound guideline, and a versatile reaction to challenges.

One of the vital manners by which self-reflection adds to inward strength is by encouraging capacity to understand individuals on a profound level. As people participate in the act of looking at their feelings, they foster an elevated aversion to the recurring pattern of their inward states. This profound education empowers people to explore their sentiments with subtlety and refinement, developing the capacity to communicate feelings usefully and figure out the feelings of others.

Besides, self-reflection goes about as a mirror, mirroring the examples of conduct and felt that shape one's reactions to outside boosts. By looking at these examples, people gain bits of knowledge into their assets and regions for development. This mindfulness is instrumental in breaking liberated from self-restricting convictions and imbued propensities that might thwart self-awareness. As people stand up to these examples head-on, they leave on an excursion of change that adds to the stronghold of their internal identities.

During the time spent self-reflection, people frequently stand up to the shadow parts of their characters — the covered up, less recognized features that might incorporate apprehensions, uncertainties, or unsettled injuries. Standing up to these shadow components is a gutsy undertaking that requires an eagerness to dive into distress. Nonetheless, it is exactly through this conflict that people gain a significant feeling of internal strength. By recognizing and incorporating these shadow viewpoints, people recover lost sections of themselves, cultivating a more comprehensive and strong self-character.

The force of self-appearance in developing inward fortitude is clear in its job as a compass for adjusting activities to values. At the point when people carve out opportunity to ponder their center convictions and values, they gain clearness on the main thing to them. This lucidity turns into a directing power that coordinates their activities and choices. The arrangement of activities with values makes a feeling of genuineness and uprightness, strengthening the internal center with a resolute obligation to rules that endure outer tensions.

Self-reflection likewise assumes a critical part in creating versatility — the ability to return from difficulty. At the point when people participate in contemplation during testing times, they gain experiences into their survival techniques, profound reactions, and critical thinking draws near. This mindfulness turns into a repository of solidarity during troublesome minutes, permitting people to draw upon their inward assets and explore misfortune with a feeling of direction and flexibility.

Besides, the act of self-reflection encourages a development mentality — a faith in the potential for learning and improvement. As people consider their encounters, the two victories and disappointments, they remove significant examples. This constant educational experience develops a mentality that perspectives challenges as any open doors for development as opposed to unrealistic snags. A development mentality adds to internal strength by ingraining versatility, flexibility, and a proactive way to deal with self-awareness.

In the domain of connections, self-reflection fills in as an impetus for developing solid associations. By analyzing one's correspondence style, social examples, and close to home triggers, people gain experiences into the elements of their associations with others. This mindfulness adds to the improvement of powerful relational abilities, sympathy, and the capacity to lay out limits — all fundamental parts of building strong and satisfying connections.

Moreover, self-reflection sustains self-empathy, an essential part of inward strength. The course of contemplation frequently includes facing one's blemishes, missteps, and weaknesses. As opposed to capitulating to self-analysis, people who practice self-reflection with a humane outlook approach their inadequacies with understanding and thoughtfulness. This self-empathy turns into a wellspring of flexibility, empowering people to climate mishaps without incorporating a feeling of disgracefulness.

Chasing after internal strength, the force of self-reflection lies in its capacity to uncover the interconnectedness of brain, body, and soul. As people investigate the profundities of their viewpoints and feelings, they become receptive to the signs radiating from their actual bodies. This brain body association cultivates an all encompassing way to deal with prosperity, perceiving that internal strength isn't exclusively a psychological develop however an amicable mix of mental, profound, and actual flexibility.

Developing inward strength through self-reflection likewise includes the affirmation and festivity of accomplishments, regardless of how little. By consistently perceiving and certifying individual achievements, people construct a positive mental self portrait and support a feeling of capability. This encouraging feedback adds to internal strength by cultivating a mentality of self-viability — the confidence in one's capacity to defeat difficulties and accomplish objectives.

The extraordinary capability of self-reflection is enhanced when people integrate different procedures into their thoughtful practices. Journaling, as perhaps of the most open and flexible technique, gives an organized stage to self-investigation. Through journaling, people can archive their contemplations, feelings, and encounters, revealing examples and acquiring clearness on their inward scenes. The put down account turns into a substantial demonstration of self-improvement, filling in as a guide for the excursion to internal strength.

Care contemplation is another procedure that synergizes with self-reflection to improve inward strength. Care includes developing present-second mindfulness without judgment. By integrating care into the act of self-reflection, people foster the capacity to notice their considerations and feelings with separation. This non-receptive mindfulness turns into a wellspring of internal strength, permitting people to answer circumstances with lucidity and self-control.

Representation methods, directed symbolism, and inventive articulation likewise add to the complex methodology of self-reflection. Through these techniques, people can get to the more profound layers of their psyche minds, disclosing wants, fears, and goals that might lie underneath the surface. Innovative articulation turns into a type of emblematic correspondence with oneself, cultivating a significant comprehension that rises above the restrictions of verbal enunciation.

In the excursion to develop inward fortitude, embracing the repeating idea of self-reflection is fundamental. The interaction is definitely not a straight direction yet a ceaseless twisting of investigation, disclosure, and reconciliation. Each pattern of self-reflection develops the groundworks of inward strength, permitting people to explore the intricacies of existence with a flexibility that rises above transitory difficulties.

It is critical to perceive that developing internal fortitude through self-reflection is definitely not a single undertaking. The help of a tutor, specialist, or a believed friend can intensify the extraordinary effect of thoughtfulness. Taking part in significant discussions around one's appearance with others cultivates a feeling of association and gives different points of view that enhance the self-revelation process.

As people leave on the excursion of self-reflection, embracing weakness turns into a foundation of internal strength. Opening oneself to the profundity of contemplation requires fortitude — the boldness to confront awkward bits of insight, to challenge instilled convictions, and to embrace the vulnerabilities that go with self-revelation. In weakness, people find flexibility, credibility, and a steady groundwork that endures the everyday hardships.

Internal strength, that elusive repository of versatility, courage, and confidence, is a quality that enables people to explore life's difficulties with effortlessness and assurance. It's anything but a decent quality however a dynamic and developing part of the human experience, molded by self-improvement, self-disclosure, and the purposeful development of one's internal assets. Developing inward fortitude is a groundbreaking excursion that includes self-reflection, the improvement of ways of dealing with hardship or stress, cultivating positive outlook moves, and embracing the interconnected components of mental, close to home, and actual prosperity.

At the core of developing internal fortitude lies the significant act of self-reflection. This deliberate interaction includes searching internally to investigate the forms of one's viewpoints, feelings, and ways of behaving.

Self-reflection is a cognizant respite in the frantic speed of life, making a space for people to dig into the complexities of their internal universes. It is in this pensive space that the underpinnings of inward strength are laid.

Through self-reflection, people gain an uplifted mindfulness — a comprehension of their assets, shortcomings, values, and inspirations. This mindfulness turns into a compass, directing people in adjusting their activities to their fundamental beliefs. At the point when there is rationality between one's qualities and activities, a feeling of genuineness arises, invigorating the internal center with a significant and versatile trustworthiness.

Besides, self-reflection fills in as a mirror, uncovering the examples and stories that shape one's discernments and reactions to the world. By inspecting these examples, people can distinguish self-restricting convictions, imbued propensities, and neglected possibilities. This mindfulness turns into the impetus for self-awareness, as people effectively participate in destroying boundaries and growing their abilities.

During the time spent self-reflection, people frequently face the shadow parts of their characters — the angles that are less recognized or even denied. These may incorporate feelings of trepidation, weaknesses, or unsettled injuries. Defying these shadow components is a demonstration of boldness that contributes fundamentally to internal strength. By recognizing and coordinating these shadow perspectives, people recover lost pieces of themselves, cultivating a more comprehensive and strong self-personality.

The act of self-reflection likewise sustains the capacity to understand people on a deeper level — a vital part of inward strength. The capacity to appreciate people on a profound level includes the capacity to perceive, comprehend, and deal with one's own feelings, as well as explore relational elements successfully. As people take part in reflection, they gain experiences into the subtleties of their close to home scene. This close to home education engages them to answer difficulties with profound flexibility and to develop positive and useful connections.

A basic part of developing internal fortitude is creating flexibility — the ability to return from misfortune. Strength isn't tied in with staying away from hardships however turning around them with versatility and constancy. Through self-reflection during testing times, people gain experiences into their survival techniques, close to home reactions, and critical thinking draws near. This mindfulness turns into a repository of solidarity during troublesome minutes, permitting people to draw upon their internal assets and explore misfortune with a feeling of direction and versatility.

Notwithstanding self-reflection, the deliberate development of survival techniques assumes a significant part in developing internal fortitude. Survival techniques are the systems people use to oversee pressure, affliction, and the intricacies of life. These components can be versatile or maladaptive, and their viability frequently relies upon mindfulness and purposefulness.

Sound ways of dealing with hardship or stress incorporate looking for social help, participating in active work, rehearsing care or unwinding procedures, and embracing a positive outlook. Social help, specifically, goes about as a strong cushion against pressure. Building an organization of steady connections upgrades strength, giving a feeling of association and a wellspring of support during testing times.

Then again, maladaptive survival techniques, for example, substance misuse, aversion, or unfortunate idealism, may give brief help however can add to long haul difficulties. Self-reflection assumes a critical part in recognizing and changing maladaptive survival strategies into better other options. It includes a genuine assessment of one's survival methods, an investigation of their fundamental inspirations, and a cognizant work to supplant unsafe propensities with productive ones.

A positive outlook is a foundation of inward strength. It includes developing a hopeful viewpoint, rethinking difficulties as any open doors for development, and keeping a confidence in one's capacity to conquer hardships. The deliberate act of appreciation is a strong device for encouraging a positive outlook. Appreciation journaling, where people consistently think about things they are grateful for, shifts the concentration based on the thing is missing to what is bountiful in their lives. This change in context adds to a versatile and engaged outlook.

Furthermore, the force of confirmations ought to be considered carefully in the mission for internal strength. Confirmations are positive articulations that people rehash to themselves, supporting wanted convictions and perspectives. When created purposefully and rehashed reliably, insistences can reshape thought designs, improve confidence, and add to a positive and enabled mentality.

Care rehearses, like reflection and careful breathing, supplement the development of internal strength by encouraging present-second mindfulness. Care includes focusing on contemplations and sentiments without judgment, permitting people to answer circumstances with lucidity and self-restraint. Care rehearses likewise advance a more profound comprehension of oneself, adding to the capacity to understand people at their core and strength.

The interconnected elements of mental, close to home, and actual prosperity are vital to developing complete internal fortitude. Mental and profound strength, sustained through self-reflection, survival techniques, and a positive outlook, are firmly interwoven with actual prosperity. Normal actual work, a fair eating routine, and sufficient rest contribute essentially to by and large versatility and internal strength.

Work out, specifically, has been displayed to have various advantages for psychological wellness. It lessens pressure chemicals, discharges endorphins (the body's regular state of mind lifters), and works on mental capability. Participating in active work likewise gives a productive outlet to push and a feeling of achievement, adding to a good mental self view.

Sufficient rest is one more fundamental part of developing internal fortitude. Quality rest is related with further developed state of mind, improved mental capability, and better pressure the board. The body and psyche go through significant cycles of fix and solidification during rest, making it a non-debatable part of by and large prosperity.

Sustenance assumes a part in actual wellbeing as well as in mental and close to home prosperity. A reasonable eating routine that incorporates different supplements upholds mind capability and adds to close to home security. Hydration, frequently neglected, is likewise fundamental for ideal mental and profound working.

The all encompassing way to deal with developing internal fortitude includes perceiving the interconnectedness of these aspects and cultivating an amicable equilibrium among them. A strong and enabled individual is one who perceives the harmonious connection between psyche, body, and feelings and finds a way deliberate ways to support every viewpoint.

One more element of developing internal fortitude is the acknowledgment of one's qualities and the arrangement of life decisions with those qualities. Values are the core values that provide life significance and motivation. At the point when people know about their basic beliefs and pursue choices that line up with them, a significant feeling of respectability and inward strength arises.

Explaining and focusing on values includes self-reflection and an investigation of the main thing to a person. It requires a cognizant assessment of convictions, yearnings, and the rules that guide navigation. This course of values explanation gives a strong groundwork to developing internal fortitude, as people can draw upon their qualities as a wellspring of inspiration and direction during testing times.

Besides, developing internal fortitude includes embracing change and vulnerability as inborn parts of life. The capacity to adjust and flourish notwithstanding change is a demonstration of internal flexibility. Self-reflection adds to this flexibility by cultivating an outlook that perspectives change not as a danger but rather as a chance for development.

The purposeful development of a development outlook, an idea created by clinician Song Dweck, is key to developing inward fortitude. A development mentality includes the conviction that capacities and insight can be created through commitment and difficult work. People with a development outlook view moves as any open doors to learn and develop, instead of as outlandish snags.

Conversely, a decent outlook, which expects that capacities are intrinsic and unchangeable, can block the improvement of inward strength. People with a decent outlook might keep away from difficulties to safeguard their mental self view, dreading disappointment as an impression of their inborn capacities.

Self-reflection assumes a urgent part in moving from a decent mentality to a development outlook by testing restricting convictions and embracing a viewpoint of consistent learning and improvement.

Chapter 4

Cultivating Resilience

Developing flexibility is an extraordinary and dynamic cycle that engages people to explore the intricacies of existence with strength, versatility, and backbone. Flexibility isn't simply the capacity to get through affliction however the ability to return, learn, and develop from testing encounters. This diverse excursion includes creating mental, close to home, and actual flexibility, encouraging a positive outlook, constructing an encouraging group of people, and embracing taking care of oneself practices.

At the core of developing strength lies the acknowledgment of the interconnected components of prosperity. Mental flexibility includes creating mental and profound techniques to adapt to pressure and difficulty. Close to home strength involves understanding and dealing with one's feelings actually. Actual flexibility envelops keeping a sound body and way of life that upholds by and large prosperity. The cooperative energy of these aspects adds to a powerful and far reaching versatility.

Building mental flexibility includes creating mental methodologies to really explore difficulties and misfortunes. One of the vital parts of mental flexibility is developing a development outlook — a conviction that difficulties are valuable open doors for learning and development. Clinician Ditty Dweck begat the expression "development mentality" to depict a demeanor that embraces difficulties, perseveres notwithstanding misfortunes, and perspectives exertion as a way to dominance.

People with a development mentality approach provokes with interest and a readiness to learn. They comprehend that capacities can be created through commitment and difficult work, and misfortunes are not demonstrative of innate limits. Developing a development mentality includes self-reflection, testing self-restricting convictions, and reexamining difficulties as any open doors for individual and expert turn of events.

One more part of mental versatility is creating mental adaptability — the capacity to adjust and move one's point of view in light of evolving conditions. Mental adaptability empowers people to explore vulnerability, think about elective perspectives, and issue address successfully. Care rehearses, like contemplation and careful

55

breathing, add to mental adaptability by cultivating present-second mindfulness and non-receptive perception of considerations.

Also, building mental strength includes creating successful pressure the board abilities. Stress is an inescapable piece of life, and what people answer pressure incredibly means for their flexibility.

Stress the executives strategies might incorporate using time productively, putting forth reasonable objectives, focusing on errands, and rehearsing unwinding procedures. Participating in exercises that give pleasure, unwinding, and a feeling of achievement likewise adds to mental flexibility.

Close to home strength is one more essential component of developing generally versatility. Profound flexibility includes perceiving, understanding, and dealing with one's own feelings really. It is the capacity to return quickly from profound misfortunes, remain grounded even with difficulty, and explore the intricacies of connections.

A critical part of close to home flexibility is the capacity to appreciate people on a profound level — the capacity to perceive and grasp both one's own feelings and the feelings of others. The capacity to appreciate anyone on a profound level includes mindfulness, self-guideline, sympathy, and viable relational correspondence. Developing capacity to appreciate anyone on a deeper level through self-reflection, undivided attention, and compassionate figuring out upgrades profound strength.

Besides, building close to home flexibility requires the capacity to adapt to and adjust to change. Life is innately unique, and people who can explore changes with close to home adaptability and receptiveness are better prepared to confront difficulties. Fostering a feeling of acknowledgment, permitting oneself to lament misfortunes, and embracing change as a characteristic piece of life add to close to home strength.

Positive connections and a solid encouraging group of people are significant for close to home strength. Interfacing with others, sharing encounters, and getting support cultivates a feeling of having a place and security. Fabricating and keeping up with solid connections include successful correspondence, common regard, and the eagerness to offer and get support. Social help goes about as a cradle during seasons of pressure and upgrades profound prosperity.

Actual flexibility is frequently neglected yet is a vital part of generally versatility. Actual prosperity gives the establishment to mental and profound prosperity. Normal active work, a reasonable eating routine, satisfactory rest, and taking care of oneself practices add to actual strength.

Participating in standard activity has been connected to various physical and psychological wellness benefits. Practice lessens pressure chemicals, discharges endorphins (the body's normal state of mind enhancers), and works on mental capability. It likewise advances better rest, which is fundamental for generally prosperity. Integrating active work into everyday schedules, like strolling, running, or rehearsing yoga, upgrades actual versatility.

A decent and nutritious eating routine is fundamental for keeping up with actual wellbeing and supporting mental capability. Supplement rich food sources give the energy and supplements vital for ideal physical processes, including the cerebrum. Hydration is additionally urgent for generally prosperity, as drying out can adversely affect mental execution and state of mind.

Sufficient rest is a non-debatable part of actual flexibility. Quality rest is related with further developed temperament, mental capability, and stress the board. Establishing a favorable rest climate, laying out an ordinary rest schedule, and focusing on rest add to physical and mental versatility.

Taking care of oneself practices incorporate a scope of exercises that support physical, mental, and profound prosperity. These practices might incorporate care reflection, unwinding strategies, side interests, or exercises that give pleasure and unwinding. Taking part in taking care of oneself isn't an extravagance yet an imperative part of building strength. Carving out margin for oneself, defining limits, and rehearsing self-empathy add to by and large prosperity.

Encouraging a positive mentality is a strong component of versatility. A positive mentality includes developing a hopeful standpoint, reexamining difficulties as any open doors for development, and keeping a faith in one's capacity to beat hardships. It doesn't deny the truth of difficulties yet sees them from a perspective of versatility and trust.

Appreciation rehearses assume a critical part in cultivating a positive mentality. Appreciation includes recognizing and valuing the positive parts of life, even amidst difficulties. Appreciation journaling, where people consistently consider things they are grateful for, has been displayed to improve prosperity and flexibility. This training shifts the concentration based on the thing is missing to what is plentiful in one's life.

Hopefulness, one more part of a positive outlook, includes seeing mishaps as impermanent and well defined for a specific circumstance as opposed to unavoidable and long-lasting. Hopeful people approach difficulties with a feeling of viability, trusting in their capacity to defeat hardships. Developing good faith includes testing negative idea designs, reexamining difficulties, and zeroing in on arrangements as opposed to issues.

Building strength is certainly not a singular undertaking however frequently needs the help of a local area or coach. Significant associations with others add to a feeling of having a place and make an organization of help during testing times. Participating in transparent discussions about flexibility with believed friends improves the self-disclosure process and supports the comprehension that building versatility is a common and aggregate excursion.

Besides, embracing versatility and adaptability is a major part of developing strength. Life is innately unusual, and people who can adjust to change with a feeling of transparency and adaptability are better prepared to confront difficulties. Strength includes the capacity to change objectives, plans, and points of view because of evolving conditions.

Embracing disappointments and misfortunes as any open doors for learning is necessary to developing strength. Disappointment isn't an impression of innate deficiency however a characteristic piece of the growing experience.

Versatile people view disappointments as venturing stones to progress, extricating examples, and adjusting their methodologies in like manner. Self-reflection assumes a critical part in reevaluating mishaps and removing significant experiences from difficulties.

4.1 Understanding the role of resilience in developing inner strength

Understanding the job of flexibility in creating inward strength uncovers a significant association between the capacity to endure difficulty and the development of a powerful, strong inward center. Flexibility, frequently portrayed as the ability to quickly return from difficulties, adjust to misfortune, and drive forward notwithstanding mishaps, is a unique quality that invigorates people on their excursion toward internal strength. This complicated relationship includes investigating the parts of versatility, perceiving the effect of mentality, cultivating the capacity to understand people on a profound level, exploring difficulty, and embracing the groundbreaking force of strength in molding a strong and enabled self.

At its center, versatility is a complex characteristic that incorporates mental, close to home, and social aspects. Mental versatility includes the capacity to keep a feeling of direction, hopefulness, and a development situated outlook during testing times. Close to home strength relates to the ability to explore and manage feelings actually, while social versatility includes looking for and offering help inside relational connections. Understanding the transaction of these aspects enlightens the way toward developing inward fortitude through strength.

A critical part of versatility is the outlook people embrace despite difficulty. The idea of a development outlook, presented by clinician Tune Dweck, highlights the conviction that capacities and insight can be created through devotion and exertion. Embracing a development mentality positions difficulties as any open doors for learning and development instead of impossible impediments. The development of this outlook contributes fundamentally to the improvement of internal strength, as people view difficulties as venturing stones toward individual and expert headway.

Besides, the connection among versatility and internal strength interlaces with the capacity to understand individuals on a profound level — a principal part of mindfulness and social intuition. The ability to appreciate anyone on a profound level includes perceiving, understanding, and dealing with one's own feelings, as well as seeing and impacting the feelings of others. People with high capacity to appreciate anyone on a profound level are better prepared to explore the intricacies of connections, convey really, and answer versatilely to personal difficulties.

In the domain of flexibility, the capacity to adjust and explore difficulty assumes a vital part in creating inward strength. Difficulty is an intrinsic piece of the human experience, and strength includes the ability to stand up to difficulties, gain from them, and arise more grounded. Exploring misfortune requires a mix of survival techniques, critical thinking abilities, and a development situated outlook. Strong people see mishaps not as outlandish obstructions but rather as any open doors for self-disclosure and change.

The extraordinary force of strength becomes clear when people perceive that misfortune is definitely not a straight excursion however a repetitive course of development and improvement. Each experience with affliction gives an open door to self-reflection, learning, and the refinement of survival techniques. Flexibility turns into a unique power that pushes people forward on their way toward inward strength, adding to the molding of a strong mentality and an enabled identity.

The comprehension of versatility as a dynamic and versatile cycle lines up with the idea of post-horrendous development — a peculiarity where people experience self-awareness and positive change in the outcome of difficulty. Instead of being characterized exclusively by the adverse consequence of testing encounters, strong people rise out of difficulty with an upgraded identity viability, a more profound appreciation forever, and a fortified inward purpose. This post-horrendous development highlights the groundbreaking likely intrinsic in versatility, representing its part in encouraging internal strength through the cauldron of affliction.

Besides, the job of flexibility in creating internal strength reaches out to the manner in which people see and oversee pressure. Strong people exhibit viable pressure the board by utilizing survival techniques that advance prosperity and forestall the pessimistic effect of stressors. These survival techniques might incorporate care rehearses, social help, active work, and positive reevaluating. The capacity to explore pressure versatilely adds to mental determination and the development of inward strength.

With regards to versatility, the significance of social help couldn't possibly be more significant. The associations people manufacture with others act as a fundamental wellspring of solidarity during testing times. Social help gives a feeling of having a place, consolation, and common perspective, making an organization that supports versatility. This organization turns into a foundation in the improvement of inward strength, stressing the mutual idea of versatility as people attract upon aggregate assets to explore difficulty.

In addition, the connection among versatility and internal strength unfurls with regards to self-viability — the confidence in one's capacity to impact occasions and results. Versatile people develop a healthy identity viability through their versatile reactions to challenges, seeing difficulties as sensible and inside their ability to survive. This confidence in their own viability turns into a main impetus in the improvement of inward strength, cultivating a proactive and engaged way to deal with life's intricacies.

Developing flexibility includes a powerful transaction between individual qualities and outer assets. The interior assets incorporate mental adaptability, close to home guideline, versatility, and a development outlook. Mental adaptability empowers people to change their points of view and procedures in light of evolving conditions, cultivating flexibility and a versatile outlook. Profound guideline permits people to explore the range of feelings really, forestalling the impeding effect of drawn out pressure. A development mentality encourages a proactive way to deal with difficulties, advancing a confidence in persistent learning and improvement.

Outside assets, like social help, local area associations, and admittance to assets, contribute altogether to the development of versatility. The accessibility of steady connections gives a cradle against stressors, encouraging close to home prosperity and adding to the improvement of internal strength. Local area associations make a feeling of having a place and shared personality, supporting the thought that flexibility is certainly not a lone undertaking however an aggregate excursion.

The comprehension of strength as a dynamic and multi-layered process welcomes people to embrace the repeating idea of development and improvement. Flexibility includes a constant circle of experiencing difficulties, adjusting, learning, and arising more grounded. This repetitive interaction lines up with the idea of the flexibility twisting, where each cycle extends the singular's ability to explore misfortune and adds to the continuous advancement of internal strength.

Embracing the flexibility winding requires a readiness to take part in self-reflection, gain from encounters, and effectively develop versatile reactions to challenges. Strong people approach each cycle with a feeling of receptiveness, perceiving that difficulty holds the potential for development and self-disclosure. This iterative cycle turns into an extraordinary excursion toward the improvement of inward strength, outlining that flexibility is certainly not a proper characteristic yet a unique quality that develops over the long run.

In the journey for inward strength, the job of flexibility turns out to be especially piercing notwithstanding existential difficulties and vulnerabilities. Existential versatility includes wrestling with significant inquiries regarding the importance of life, the idea of human life, and the quest for a deliberate and true life. Strong people explore existential difficulties by embracing vulnerability, looking for importance in their encounters, and developing a feeling of direction that rises above flitting challenges.

Existential flexibility highlights the significance of adjusting one's activities to profoundly held values and convictions. At the point when people defy existential inquiries, they draw upon their internal stores of strength to explore the intricacies of direction and significance. The capacity to find significance in misfortune adds to the improvement of internal strength, as people anchor themselves in a reason that rises above the transient idea of difficulties.

All in all, understanding the job of flexibility in creating internal strength uncovers a significant and interconnected excursion of development, variation, and self-disclosure. Flexibility isn't simply a reaction to difficulty however an extraordinary cycle that shapes the inward scene of people, cultivating a versatile outlook, the capacity to understand individuals on a deeper level, and the capacity to explore difficulties with strength and elegance. The repetitive idea of versatility, the groundbreaking capability of post-horrendous development, and the common parts of social help feature the powerful interchange among flexibility and the improvement of inward strength.

Embracing flexibility as a dynamic and developing quality welcomes people to see difficulties as any open doors for development, perceive the extraordinary force of misfortune, and leave on an excursion toward a versatile and enabled identity.

4.2 Strategies for building resilience in the face of challenges

Techniques for building versatility even with difficulties incorporate a scope of proactive methodologies that enable people to explore difficulty, return from mishaps, and develop a powerful internal center. Versatility, the capacity to adjust and flourish notwithstanding hardships, is a unique quality that can be created and fortified over the long run. These techniques include encouraging a development mentality, improving capacity to understand people at their core, developing social encouraging groups of people, rehearsing taking care of oneself, embracing idealism, and creating critical thinking abilities. The collaboration of these procedures adds to the all encompassing advancement of flexibility and outfits people with the instruments to confront life's difficulties with versatility and assurance.

At the center of building strength is the development of a development mentality — an essential conviction that difficulties are open doors for learning and development. This outlook, proposed by clinician Tune Dweck, includes seeing mishaps not as signs of inborn limits but rather as venturing stones toward individual and expert turn of events. People with a development mentality approach difficulties with interest, an eagerness to learn, and a comprehension that work is a way to dominance.

To cultivate a development outlook, people can participate in self-reflection to distinguish and challenge fixed convictions about capacities and knowledge. This cycle includes looking at thought designs, reevaluating negative self-talk, and embracing difficulties with a feeling of interest as opposed to fear. Through deliberate endeavors to take on a development outlook, people establish the groundwork for flexibility, as they see misfortunes as any open doors for self-revelation and persistent improvement.

Improving ability to understand anyone at their core is one more key technique in building versatility. The ability to appreciate people on a profound level includes perceiving, understanding, and dealing with one's own feelings, as well as seeing and impacting the feelings of others. Tough people explore difficulties with close to home mindfulness, manage their feelings successfully, and participate in compassionate correspondence.

Rehearsing the ability to appreciate individuals at their core starts with mindfulness — a legit affirmation and comprehension of one's own feelings. Ordinary self-reflection, journaling, and care rehearses add to uplifted profound mindfulness. This mindfulness turns into the anchor for close to home guideline, as people figure out how to oversee pressure, nervousness, and other testing feelings in valuable ways.

Additionally, creating sympathy and compelling relational abilities are fundamental parts of the capacity to understand people on a profound level. Strong people comprehend their own feelings as well as sympathize with the sensations of others. Developing sympathy includes undivided attention, viewpoint taking, and looking to grasp the feelings basic others' ways of behaving. Solid relational abilities empower people to articulate their thoughts decisively, construct positive connections, and look for help when required.

Building strength is certainly not a single undertaking yet frequently includes the help of an informal organization. Developing social encouraging groups of people is a significant technique for strength, giving people a feeling of having a place, support, and common perspective. These organizations go about as a cradle during seasons of pressure, offering consistent encouragement, viable help, and different viewpoints.

To fabricate social encouraging groups of people, people can put time and exertion in supporting existing connections and shaping new associations. Open correspondence, shared trust, and correspondence are fundamental components of solid connections that add to the advancement of flexibility. Taking part in friendly exercises, taking an interest in bunch exercises or clubs, and searching out similar people set out open doors for significant associations.

In the midst of affliction, connecting for help and communicating weakness are demonstrations of solidarity that develop social associations. Strong people perceive the significance of shared encounters, permitting them to draw upon the aggregate insight and assets of their informal communities. Building strength through friendly help includes both giving and getting support, making a complementary and supporting powerful inside the organization.

Taking care of oneself practices are crucial techniques for building strength, stressing the significance of keeping up with physical, mental, and close to home prosperity. Taking care of oneself includes purposeful activities that focus on one's wellbeing and joy, perceiving that a versatile individual requires major areas of strength for an of generally prosperity. Normal taking care of oneself adds to pressure decrease, close to home guideline, and the conservation of mental and actual energy.

Taking care of oneself practices differ for every person, enveloping exercises that give pleasure, unwinding, and a feeling of satisfaction. These may incorporate activity, care contemplation, imaginative pursuits, perusing, investing energy in nature, or taking part in side interests. The key is to distinguish exercises that reverberate with individual inclinations and add to a feeling of equilibrium and restoration.

Notwithstanding individual taking care of oneself works on, cultivating strength likewise includes making a steady and sound way of life. This incorporates keeping a reasonable eating regimen, focusing on customary actual work, guaranteeing sufficient rest, and overseeing pressure through unwinding strategies.

The interconnected elements of physical, mental, and profound prosperity structure the reason for building flexibility through far reaching taking care of oneself practices.

Embracing good faith is a strong mental system for building strength. Confidence includes keeping an uplifting perspective, rethinking difficulties as any open doors, and trusting in one's capacity to beat challenges. Strong people approach misfortunes with a hopeful outlook, seeing them as brief and intended for a specific circumstance instead of unavoidable and extremely durable.

Developing hopefulness includes testing negative idea designs and developing positive confirmations. People can take part in mental rebuilding, which includes recognizing and testing pessimistic programmed contemplations and supplanting them with additional positive and productive ones. Confirmations, or positive self-proclamations, build up hopeful convictions and add to a versatile mentality.

Besides, creating critical thinking abilities is a fundamental procedure for building flexibility. Strong people approach difficulties with a proactive and arrangement centered outlook, perceiving that powerful critical thinking adds to versatile reactions. Critical thinking includes separating difficulties into sensible advances, laying out reasonable objectives, and recognizing expected arrangements.

To improve critical thinking abilities, people can utilize methodical methodologies, for example, the critical thinking model. This model includes characterizing the issue, creating likely arrangements, assessing the advantages and disadvantages of every arrangement, choosing the best strategy, and executing and assessing the picked arrangement. By creating compelling critical thinking abilities, people fabricate trust in their capacity to explore difficulties and add to the improvement of versatility.

Furthermore, embracing a feeling of direction and significance is a system that strengthens flexibility despite challenges. An unmistakable feeling of direction gives people a directing compass that rises above transient challenges, adding to the improvement of internal strength. Distinguishing individual qualities, explaining long haul objectives, and adjusting activities to a feeling of direction make a versatile establishment that endures the trial of misfortune.

The joining of care rehearses into day to day existence is a groundbreaking methodology for building flexibility. Care includes developing present-second mindfulness, non-critical perception of considerations and feelings, and acknowledgment of the ongoing experience. Care rehearses, like reflection and careful breathing, add to profound guideline, stress decrease, and the improvement of a strong mentality.

Tough people take part in care as a device for exploring difficulties with clearness and levelheadedness. The act of care permits people to answer stressors in a quiet and conscious way, forestalling receptive and imprudent reactions.

By cultivating a profound comprehension of oneself and the current second, care adds to the improvement of strength as people explore the intricacies of existence with more prominent poise.

Besides, reevaluating difficulties as any open doors for development is a mental technique that improves strength. Strong people decipher misfortunes as important growth opportunities, rethinking difficulty as an impetus for individual and expert turn of events. This mental shift includes seeing difficulties with a feeling of interest, perceiving the potential for self-revelation and change.

To consolidate this procedure, people can take part in mental rebuilding by testing pessimistic idea designs related with difficulty. By addressing programmed negative considerations and taking on an additional fair and valuable viewpoint, people encourage flexibility and embrace difficulties as fundamental components of their development process. Rethinking difficulties as any open doors builds up a positive and engaged outlook.

4.3 Inspirational stories of individuals who have overcome adversity through resilience

In the immense embroidery of human experience, motivational accounts of people beating difficulty through versatility act as encouraging signs, exhibiting the phenomenal limit of the human soul to transcend difficulties. These stories enlighten the groundbreaking force of flexibility, displaying how people explore misfortune, quickly return from mishaps, and arise more grounded, savvier, and more engaged. These accounts are a demonstration of the unstoppable will that dwells inside every individual, a power that can transform preliminaries into wins and mishaps into venturing stones. Here, we investigate a few such rousing stories that feature the noteworthy versatility showed by people despite different difficulties.

One convincing account of versatility is the narrative of Malala Yousafzai, a Pakistani extremist for female training who resisted the Taliban and endure a close deadly gunfire wound. Brought into the world in the Smack Valley of Pakistan, Malala was a backer for young ladies' schooling since early on, contributing to a blog for the BBC Urdu under a nom de plume. Nonetheless, her activism got under the skin of the Taliban, who designated her for pushing schooling for young ladies.

In October 2012, a Taliban shooter boarded Malala's school transport and shot her in the head. Wonderfully, Malala endure the assault and, with steadfast strength, proceeded with her promotion for young ladies' schooling on a worldwide scale. Her striking process, set apart by fortitude and a resolute obligation to her goal, finished in Malala turning into the most youthful ever beneficiary of the Nobel Harmony Prize in 2014.

Malala's story embodies the strength that arises notwithstanding grave difficulty. Her unfaltering commitment to schooling and orientation equity, even in the outcome of a perilous assault, fills in as a strong demonstration of the extraordinary capability of strength. Malala won over private misfortune as well as turned into an image of expectation and motivation for innumerable others confronting their difficulties.

One more surprising story of flexibility is found in the existence of Scratch Vujicic, an Australian powerful orator and evangelist brought into the world with tetra-amelia condition, an uncommon problem described by the shortfall of every one of the four appendages. Notwithstanding the significant actual difficulties he confronted, Scratch's story is one of win over misfortune and the development of flexibility.

Growing up, Scratch experienced snapshots of sadness and mulled over self destruction because of the confinement and tormenting he persevered. Be that as it may, he tracked down strength through his confidence, family, and a steady assurance to carry on with an intentional life. Scratch figured out how to embrace his disparities as well as turned into a backer for people with incapacities.

Scratch's process took a groundbreaking turn when he found his enthusiasm for public talking. He started sharing his story, spreading a message of trust, flexibility, and the force of a positive mentality. Scratch's biography epitomizes how versatility, combined with a feeling of direction, can transform apparently outlandish difficulties into valuable open doors for individual and cultural development.

The account of J.K. Rowling, the acclaimed creator of the Harry Potter series, offers a significant delineation of versatility despite difficulty. Prior to making worldwide progress, Rowling confronted a progression of individual and expert misfortunes. As a single parent living in neediness, she fought sorrow and considered self destruction. Her original copy for the first Harry Potter book was dismissed by various distributers, adding to the difficulties she confronted.

Be that as it may, Rowling's flexibility and confidence in her story pushed her forward. She persevered in her composition regardless of dismissal, monetary battles, and individual difficulties. In the long run, her persistence paid off when the first Harry Potter book was distributed. The series proceeded to turn into a worldwide peculiarity, changing Rowling from a striving single parent to one of the world's best and powerful creators.

Rowling's story highlights the extraordinary idea of versatility and how misfortunes can prepare for phenomenal achievement. Her excursion from misfortune to win fills in as a motivation for hopeful scholars and people confronting their own difficulties, showing the way that flexibility can be an impetus for significant individual and expert development.

The narrative of Nelson Mandela, the counter politically-sanctioned racial segregation progressive and previous Leader of South Africa, is a demonstration of strength despite massive misfortune and unfairness. Mandela burned through 27 years in jail for his job in restricting the abusive politically-sanctioned racial segregation system. In spite of persevering through unforgiving circumstances and being isolated from his family, Mandela stayed undaunted in his obligation to the battle for fairness and equity.

Upon his delivery in 1990, Mandela proceeded with his battle against politically-sanctioned racial segregation, in the end prompting its destroying and the foundation of a popularity based South Africa. Mandela's versatility stretched out past his delivery from jail; he assumed a critical part in cultivating compromise and solidarity in a country profoundly isolated by many years of racial isolation.

Mandela's story epitomizes the getting through force of flexibility to beat individual difficulties as well as foundational bad form. His obligation to absolution, compromise, and country building highlights the groundbreaking capability of strength on both an individual and cultural level.

The existence of Oprah Winfrey is another story that mirrors the victory of strength over difficulty. Naturally introduced to destitution and confronting a difficult youth set apart by misuse and difficulty, Oprah's initial years were a long way from demonstrative of the worldwide news magnate she would turn into. Notwithstanding the obstructions, Oprah's versatility, assurance, and energy for narrating moved her toward a lifelong in media.

Oprah experienced various difficulties in her excursion, including being terminated from a TV commentator position. Be that as it may, she wouldn't be characterized by her difficulties. Oprah's unmatched capacity to interface with individuals, combined with her strength, prompted the making of "The Oprah Winfrey Show," which turned into an earth shattering stage for conversations on different points.

As her vocation thrived, Oprah extended her impact past TV, securing herself as a giver, maker, and persuasive figure in media outlets. Her story fills in as a reference point of versatility, outlining how an enduring obligation to self-improvement and the quest for one's interests can prompt remarkable achievement.

The account of Arunima Sinha, the primary female handicapped person to climb Mount Everest, epitomizes strength in the domain of physical and mental perseverance. Arunima, a previous public level volleyball player in India, confronted a life changing occurrence when she was tossed from a moving train while opposing a burglary. The misfortune brought about the removal of one of her legs.

Rather than capitulating to surrender, Arunima diverted her torment into an assurance to accomplish something phenomenal. She put her focus on Mount Everest, one of the world's most difficult pinnacles. Arunima's excursion to the culmination was tiring, set apart by extreme actual preparation, mental strength, and an enduring obligation to her objective.

In 2013, Arunima effectively summited Mount Everest, defeating her actual restrictions as well as motivating endless people all over the planet. Her story outlines that versatility goes past returning from difficulty; it includes a gutsy jump forward, pushing the limits of what is considered conceivable.

The existence of Steve Occupations, prime supporter of Mac Inc., is an account of flexibility, development, and the capacity to bounce back from difficulties. Regardless of being a visionary in the tech business, Occupations confronted huge difficulties all through his vocation. He was expelled from Apple, the organization he helped to establish, just to return years after the fact and lead it to extraordinary achievement.

Occupations' process was set apart by the two victories and disappointments, including the promising and less promising times of Apple's fortunes. His strength was obvious in his capacity to gain from mishaps, adjust to evolving conditions, and imagine items that changed whole ventures. Occupations' obligation to his vision, even notwithstanding misfortune, brought about noteworthy developments like the iPhone, iPad, and MacBook.

His life fills in as a demonstration of the possibility that flexibility isn't just about enduring tempests however outfitting the illustrations gained from difficulties to fuel future achievement. Occupations' story is an update that misfortunes can be venturing stones to unrivaled accomplishment, and flexibility is the main thrust behind groundbreaking development.

The story of Elizabeth Brilliant, an overcomer of a nerve racking snatching, mirrors the significant strength that can arise in the result of injury. In 2002, at 14 years old, Savvy was hijacked from her home in Utah and held hostage for a long time. During this time, she persevered through physical and psychological mistreatment, confronting unfathomable conditions.

Brilliant's capacity to get by and ultimately recover her life is a demonstration of her versatility. After her salvage, she turned into a backer for survivors of kidnapping and rape, utilizing her horrendous experience to bring issues to light about the significance of kid security. Brilliant's strength is clear in her own excursion of recuperation as well as in her obligation to enabling other people who have confronted comparable injuries.

The tale of flexibility isn't restricted to well known people; it stretches out to innumerable ordinary legends who explore individual difficulties with uncommon strength.

Think about the tale of a disease survivor who, confronted with a life changing conclusion, calls the versatility to go through treatment, face fears, and arise with a newly discovered appreciation forever. These stories highlight that versatility is a widespread quality that lives inside every individual, ready to be stirred despite misfortune.

In the domain of sports, the narrative of Michael Jordan, broadly viewed as one of the best b-ball players ever, exemplifies flexibility chasing after greatness. Jordan confronted various mishaps, including being cut from his secondary school b-ball group — a dismissal that powered his assurance to turn into the best. All through his profession, Jordan experienced difficulties, analysis, and snapshots of rout.

Nonetheless, his flexibility and persistent hard working attitude pushed him to six NBA titles, five MVP grants, and various honors. Jordan's capacity to quickly return from misfortunes, keep up with center during difficulty, and reliably lift his game has made him a persevering through image of athletic strength.

These motivational stories all in all stress the assorted appearances of flexibility and its groundbreaking effect on people from various different backgrounds. From enduring hazardous circumstances to beating individual difficulties, these accounts uncover the widespread limit with regards to versatility that exists inside the human soul.

The examples got from these accounts feature key parts of versatility:

Outlook Matters: Versatile people frequently have a development mentality, seeing difficulties as any open doors for learning and development. This mentality energizes their assurance to beat difficulty and encourages an uplifting perspective on life.

Reason and Energy Drive Strength: A large number of these people found flexibility through a solid feeling of direction or an enthusiastic pursuit. Whether supporting for a purpose, seeking after imaginative undertakings, or making progress toward individual objectives, a feeling of direction can be a strong inspiration despite challenges.

Association and Local area Backing: Social encouraging groups of people assume a vital part in versatility. Whether it's the help of family, companions, or a more extensive local area, having an organization to rest on gives profound strength and builds up a singular's ability to persevere.

Gaining from Mishaps: Strength includes the capacity to gain from difficulties, adjust to evolving conditions, and endure chasing after objectives. Misfortunes are not seen as disappointments however as venturing stones toward self-awareness and achievement.

Positive Mentality and Confidence: Strong people frequently keep a positive outlook and idealism even notwithstanding misfortune. This inspirational perspective turns into a main impetus, impacting their capacity to defeat difficulties and bounce back from misfortunes.

Versatility and Adaptability: Strength is portrayed by versatility and adaptability in answering evolving conditions. People who explore misfortune with adaptability and transparency are better prepared to track down savvy fixes and conquer hindrances.

Obligation to Self-awareness: Versatile people focus on continuous self-awareness, both concerning mindfulness and ability advancement. This responsibility energizes their ability to confront difficulties with a feeling of dominance and certainty.

Transforming Misfortune into Backing: Numerous versatile people channel their encounters of affliction into support, utilizing their accounts to bring issues to light, rouse others, and add to positive change in their networks or worldwide.

These accounts highlight that versatility is certainly not a one-size-fits-all idea yet a dynamic and developing quality that shows extraordinarily in every individual's excursion. Whether defeating actual handicaps, getting through injury, exploring vocation mishaps, or winning over cultural treacheries, the ongoing idea is the relentless soul that will not be broken by affliction.

Beating misfortune through flexibility is a significant demonstration of the strength of the human soul and its ability to persevere, adjust, and flourish notwithstanding difficulties. The accounts of people who have vanquished misfortune through flexibility act as signals of motivation, enlightening the groundbreaking influence that lives inside the human experience. This investigation dives into the diverse elements of versatility and the manners by which people explore difficulties, injury, and life changing conditions with enduring assurance, at last rising up out of the cauldron of difficulty more grounded, savvier, and more enabled.

At the core of beating affliction lies strength — a complex interaction of mental, profound, and social factors that empowers people to return from difficulties. Versatility is certainly not a static quality yet a powerful interaction that includes adapting to misfortune, adjusting to change, and developing through life's difficulties. The excursion of beating misfortune through versatility frequently starts with the development of a tough outlook — a perspective that perspectives challenges as any open doors for development and learning.

Consider the tale of Viktor Frankl, a specialist and Holocaust survivor, whose strength was manufactured in the pot of quite possibly of humankind's most obscure period. Frankl, detained in Nazi death camps during The Second Great War, got through unbelievable torment and misfortune. In any case, he found that even in the direst conditions, people have the opportunity to pick their reaction to misfortune.

Frankl's original work, "Man's Quest for Importance," investigates how people can track down reason and significance even amidst significant misery. His story shows that the flexibility to defeat difficulty starts with an outlook that rises above the outer conditions, stressing the inward opportunity to pick one's disposition and reaction.

Essentially, the existence of Aron Ralston, portrayed in the film "127 Hours," offers a convincing story of flexibility. Ralston, an enthusiastic outdoorsman, wound up caught in an Utah gorge when a stone stuck his arm. Confronted with inescapable demise and following quite a while of segregation, Ralston settled on the nerve racking choice to sever his own arm to free himself.

Ralston's story is a demonstration of the human limit with regards to versatility in the most ridiculously critical circumstances. His assurance to get by, combined with a mentality zeroed in on definitive activity, empowered him to defeat an exceptional difficulty. Ralston's experience features that flexibility frequently includes pursuing hard choices and making conclusive moves, even notwithstanding apparently outlandish difficulties.

Past individual mentality, close to home strength assumes a vital part in exploring difficulty. Close to home versatility includes the capacity to perceive, comprehend, and deal with one's feelings successfully, particularly during seasons of pressure and commotion. The narrative of Malala Yousafzai, the Pakistani lobbyist for female training, epitomizes the force of close to home flexibility notwithstanding viciousness and abuse.

Malala endure a designated assault by the Taliban for her promotion of young ladies' schooling. Her profound flexibility, portrayed by boldness, determination, and a guarantee to her objective, permitted her not exclusively to endure the actual injury yet additionally to proceed with her worldwide activism. Malala's story highlights that profound strength engages people to stand up to difficulty with a feeling of direction and assurance.

The association between close to home versatility and the capacity to conquer difficulty is additionally exemplified in the encounters of troopers getting back from disaster areas. Numerous veterans face actual wounds as well as significant profound and mental difficulties. The most common way of defeating injury and remaking their lives frequently requires a versatile close to home mentality, upheld by helpful mediations, social associations, and a feeling of direction past the war zone.

Social versatility, the third element of strength, stresses the job of social associations, local area support, and relational connections in conquering difficulty. The narrative of Amanda Lindhout, a Canadian columnist who was grabbed and held hostage in Somalia for a very long time, gives understanding into the meaning of social strength.

During her imprisonment, Lindhout tracked down strength and flexibility in framing a bond with another prisoner, Nigel Brennan. Their common encounters and shared help turned into a life saver in the midst of the unforgiving states of bondage.

After their delivery, Lindhout laid out the Worldwide Enhancement Establishment, showing the way that social strength can stretch out past private recuperation to add to the prosperity of others.

The significance of social flexibility is additionally featured in the recuperation cycle of people confronting dependence. Defeating substance misuse frequently includes reconstructing social associations, cultivating an encouraging group of people, and taking part in bunch treatment. The aggregate strength of a steady local area turns into a foundation in the excursion toward recuperation, underscoring that versatility isn't exclusively a singular undertaking yet a shared exertion.

Notwithstanding attitude and close to home and social strength, one more significant part of conquering difficulty is the capacity to adjust and embrace change. The narrative of Bethany Hamilton, an expert surfer who lost her arm in a shark assault, embodies the strength conceived out of versatility. As opposed to surrendering to the misfortune, Hamilton adjusted to her new reality, relearning how to surf and ultimately turning into a wellspring of motivation for some.

Hamilton's excursion exhibits that conquering difficulty frequently requires an eagerness to embrace change, adjust to unexpected conditions, and track down better approaches to seek after one's interests and objectives. Strength, in this specific situation, turns into a powerful course of persistent variation and development.

Moreover, the story of Elizabeth Brilliant, who endure a frightening snatching, enlightens the groundbreaking force of flexibility in recovering one's life after injury. Savvy's capacity to reintegrate into society, share her story, and promoter for casualties of kidnapping highlights the versatility that rises up out of the most common way of mending and revamping.

Beating affliction through versatility isn't exclusively about returning quickly to the pre-emergency state yet in addition about accomplishing post-awful development. The idea of post-awful development proposes that people can encounter positive mental changes and self-improvement in the repercussions of injury. This extraordinary part of versatility is clear in the tales of people who, notwithstanding getting through huge difficulties, arose with a more profound feeling of direction, sympathy, and appreciation.

The excursion of strength frequently includes a course of rethinking misfortune as a chance for self-awareness. This mental shift, exemplified in the accounts of Holocaust survivors like Viktor Frankl, includes tracking down importance and reason notwithstanding languishing. As opposed to capitulating to surrender, versatile people reevaluate their stories, seeing misfortune as an impetus for self-revelation, strength, and insight.

A remarkable instance of rethinking difficulty is found in the encounters of people living with ongoing sicknesses. Many have embraced their circumstances as any open doors for self-awareness, support, and association with others confronting comparable difficulties. This story shift from exploitation to strengthening mirrors the groundbreaking force of flexibility in exploring persistent medical issue.

The narratives of people who have defeated affliction through strength highlight that this extraordinary excursion is frequently nonlinear and described by misfortunes, backslides, and snapshots of uncertainty. Flexibility is certainly not a one-time accomplishment yet a continuous cycle that requires diligence, self-sympathy, and a guarantee to self-improvement. The recurrent idea of strength, set apart by ceaseless transformation and learning, is exemplified in the tales of the people who explore misfortune with versatility.

In addition, the idea of strength reaches out past individual accounts to aggregate encounters, accentuating the job of networks, societies, and social orders in defeating difficulty. The aggregate versatility showed in the repercussions of catastrophic events, pandemics, or social disturbances represents how networks can meet up to revamp, support one another, and encourage a common feeling of strength.

For example, the flexibility of networks confronting the fallout of Tropical storm Katrina or the continuous difficulties introduced by the Coronavirus pandemic mirrors an aggregate strength that rises above individual encounters. The interconnectedness of social strength becomes clear as networks join to offer help, assets, and a feeling of having a place during times.

Chapter 5

Nurturing Positive Habits

Sustaining positive propensities is an excursion that unfurls in the day to day embroidery of our lives. A guarantee to encouraging ways of behaving add to our prosperity, self-awareness, and in general joy. While the street to developing positive propensities might appear to be testing, the prizes are significant and sweeping. This excursion requires mindfulness, discipline, and a certified longing for positive change.

At the center of supporting positive propensities is the comprehension that propensities shape our lives. Our everyday schedules, rehashed activities, and decisions aggregate to shape the texture of our reality. Consequently, deliberately developing propensities that line up with our qualities and objectives can prompt a really satisfying and intentional life.

One critical part of sustaining positive propensities is perceiving the force of consistency. Propensities are shaped through reiteration, and the predictable act of positive ways of behaving changes them into imbued propensities. Whether it's taking on a customary work-out daily schedule, developing a care practice, or focusing on smart dieting, consistency is the bedrock whereupon positive propensities are fabricated.

In the domain of self-improvement, positive propensities act as the structure blocks for enduring change. These propensities incorporate a wide range of exercises, from the physical to the psychological and close to home. Participating in standard activity, keeping a sound eating regimen, rehearsing care, and cultivating positive connections are instances of propensities that add to comprehensive prosperity.

Actual wellbeing is a foundation of a positive and dynamic life. Standard activity works on actual wellness as well as improves mental lucidity and close to home prosperity. The body and psyche are complicatedly associated, and the positive effect of activity resounds through each aspect of our being. It's about the outside appearance as well as about the inside imperativeness that comes from a very much sustained actual state.

Nourishment, as well, assumes a significant part in supporting positive propensities. The food we devour is the fuel for our bodies and brains. Embracing a fair and nutritious eating regimen is a propensity that delivers profits as far as energy levels, mental capability, and in general wellbeing. Settling on careful decisions about what we eat is a vital piece of the excursion towards a better way of life.

Chasing positive propensities, the brain is a strong partner and, on occasion, an impressive foe. Developing mental flexibility and cultivating a positive outlook are propensities that can fundamentally influence the nature of our lives. Care and contemplation rehearses offer instruments for restraining the fretful brain, advancing profound equilibrium, and developing a profound feeling of internal harmony.

Positive propensities reach out past the person to envelop our connections with others. Constructing and sustaining positive connections is a propensity that contributes incomprehensibly to our social and profound prosperity. Correspondence, compassion, and authentic association are fundamental parts of cultivating solid connections. These propensities enhance our lives as well as make a gradually expanding influence, impacting the prosperity of everyone around us.

The computerized age has carried with it another arrangement of difficulties and open doors in the domain of propensities. Overseeing screen time, developing a solid relationship with innovation, and being aware of our web-based communications are arising as fundamental propensities in the cutting edge period. Finding some kind of harmony between the virtual and the genuine, and being purposeful about our computerized propensities, is vital for keeping a sound and satisfying way of life.

As we explore the intricacies of current life, using time productively turns into a basic part of supporting positive propensities. Successfully focusing on errands, defining sensible objectives, and pursuing time-obstructing are routines that engage us to take full advantage within recent memory. By deliberately distributing time to exercises that line up with our qualities, we make an establishment for a reason driven and satisfying life.

The working environment is a huge field for the statement of propensities, and sustaining positive work propensities is instrumental in profession achievement and individual fulfillment. Industriousness, incredible skill, successful correspondence, and a promise to constant learning are propensities that add to a flourishing and satisfying proficient life. Besides, developing a positive work culture and cultivating solid associations with partners are propensities that improve both individual and aggregate prosperity.

The excursion of sustaining positive propensities isn't without its snags. Defeating stalling, overseeing pressure, and exploring misfortunes are innate difficulties on this way. Be that as it may, these difficulties likewise present open doors for development and self-disclosure. Creating flexibility notwithstanding affliction and gaining from difficulties are propensities that invigorate our personality and add to long haul achievement.

Reflection and mindfulness are fundamental parts of the propensity sustaining venture. Getting some margin for thoughtfulness, setting expectations, and consistently evaluating our advancement are propensities that keep us lined up with our objectives.

Through mindfulness, we gain bits of knowledge into our inspirations, values, and regions for development. This mindfulness turns into a compass directing us on the way to self-awareness and positive propensity development.

The social and social setting where we exist impacts the propensities we structure. Social standards, cultural assumptions, and friend impacts shape the scene of our day to day decisions. Supporting positive propensities requires a cognizant assessment of these impacts and an eagerness to graph our own course. It includes embracing propensities that reverberate with our bona fide selves, regardless of whether they wander from winning standards.

Nurturing and schooling assume urgent parts in molding propensities since early on. Imparting positive propensities in kids includes demonstrating ways of behaving, encouraging a development mentality, and giving a strong climate to investigation and learning. Instruction, both formal and casual, is a vehicle for communicating values and imparting propensities that add to individual and cultural prosperity.

Chasing after sure propensities, the job of inspiration couldn't possibly be more significant. Inspiration fills in as the main impetus behind propensity development and supports our obligation to positive change. Understanding the wellsprings of inspiration, whether characteristic or outward, enables us to develop propensities that line up with our qualities and desires. Besides, inspiration is definitely not a static power; it requires standard energizing through motivation, objective setting, and a feeling of direction.

As we dig into the complexities of propensity arrangement, the idea of propensity circles comes to the very front. Propensity circles comprise of a sign, daily schedule, and prize. Distinguishing the signals that trigger undesired propensities and supplanting them with positive schedules is a vital technique in propensity change. The prizes related with positive propensities support their reiteration, hardening them in our day to day routines.

Responsibility and backing are significant components in the propensity supporting cycle. Imparting our objectives to other people, looking for mentorship, and building an encouraging group of people establish a climate that energizes positive propensity development. The excursion turns out to be more pleasant and economical when we have partners who comprehend and uphold our yearnings.

In the consistently developing scene of self-awareness, remaining versatile is a crucial propensity. Adaptability notwithstanding change, receptiveness to groundbreaking thoughts, and an eagerness to recalibrate our propensities add to versatility and long haul achievement. The capacity to gain from encounters, turn when fundamental, and embrace the development attitude is characteristic for the propensity supporting excursion.

The coordination of innovation into our day to day routines has opened new roads for propensity arrangement. Portable applications, wearables, and online networks offer devices and assets to track and support positive propensities. From wellness applications that screen work-out schedules to reflection applications that guide care rehearses, innovation fills in as a sidekick on the propensity sustaining venture. Notwithstanding, careful utilization of innovation is fundamental to forestall its likely traps, for example, unnecessary screen time and computerized interruption.

Chasing positive propensities, the idea of cornerstone propensities is essential. Cornerstone propensities are urgent ways of behaving that have a flowing impact, affecting different parts of our lives. Distinguishing and sustaining cornerstone propensities can be an essential way to deal with starting positive change. For instance, customary activity, frequently thought to be a cornerstone propensity, adds to actual wellbeing as well as impacts state of mind, efficiency, and in general prosperity.

The interconnectedness of propensities features the all encompassing nature of self-improvement. Sustaining positive propensities isn't bound to disconnected ways of behaving; rather, it includes a thorough methodology that tends to the physical, mental, profound, social, and otherworldly components of our lives. Coordinating propensities across these aspects makes an agreeable and feasible starting point for a satisfying life.

In the fabulous embroidery of propensity development, the idea of resolution holds a critical spot. Determination is the power that empowers us to oppose prompt allurements for long haul objectives. While self discipline is a limited asset that can be drained, it can likewise be reinforced through training and adjustment. Creating propensities that moderate and recharge resolve, like satisfactory rest and stress the executives, adds to supported poise.

The excursion of sustaining positive propensities is a continuous interaction, set apart by persistent development and advancement. It requires persistence, self-empathy, and a readiness to embrace blemish. The way isn't direct, and mishaps are inescapable. Nonetheless, seeing mishaps as any open doors for learning and change rethinks difficulties as venturing stones instead of hindrances.

In the domain of positive propensities, the force of ceremonies can't be neglected. Ceremonies give a feeling of construction, importance, and progression in our lives. Whether a morning schedule establishes the vibe for the afternoon or a sleep time custom that advances unwinding, integrating significant ceremonies into our day to day routines adds a layer of deliberateness to our propensities.

The idea of deliberate living converges with the propensity sustaining venture. Deliberate living includes adjusting our activities to our qualities and intentionally picking how we invest our significant investment.

An intentional way to deal with life stresses reason, care, and satisfaction. Sustaining positive propensities is a foundation of purposeful living, as it includes settling on decisions that add to our general prosperity and long haul objectives.

In the domain of positive propensities, the impact of the climate is significant. Our actual environmental factors, groups of friends, and social setting shape the setting in which propensities are framed. Establishing a climate that upholds positive propensities includes planning spaces that work with wanted ways of behaving, encircling ourselves with positive impacts, and developing a culture that values prosperity.

The idea of propensity stacking is a reasonable methodology for integrating new propensities into existing schedules. By connecting another propensity with a laid out one, we influence the force of a current daily schedule to work with the reception of another way of behaving. Propensity stacking is a logical methodology that improves on the course of propensity development and upgrades the probability of progress.

As we explore the propensity supporting excursion, the significance of taking care of oneself becomes clear. Taking care of oneself is a comprehensive practice that incorporates physical, profound, and mental prosperity. It includes paying attention to our necessities, defining limits, and focusing on exercises that recharge and revive. Supporting positive propensities is a demonstration of taking care of oneself, as it includes putting resources into ways of behaving that add to our drawn out wellbeing and bliss.

The job of propensities in molding our character is a significant part of the propensity sustaining venture. Our propensities are not simply activities; they are articulations of what our identity is and who we seek to turn into. Supporting positive propensities includes adjusting our propensities to our qualities and making a personality that mirrors our true self. It's an excursion of self-revelation and self-articulation through deliberate activities.

Chasing positive propensities, the idea of time dominance is vital. Time dominance includes overseeing time as well as utilizing it as an asset for individual and expert development. It's tied in with laying out boundaries, pursuing cognizant decisions, and augmenting the utilization of time for exercises that line up with our objectives. Time authority is a fundamental propensity that enables us to lead intentional and satisfying lives.

In the excellent woven artwork of propensity development, the impact of normal practices and social accounts is huge. Cultural assumptions, social qualities, and winning standards shape the scene inside which propensities are developed. Supporting positive propensities might include testing cultural standards that don't line up with our qualities and fashioning our own way. It requires a degree of mental fortitude and conviction to break liberated from the impact of outer assumptions and outline a course directed by interior standards.

The excursion of supporting positive propensities is characteristically attached to the idea of self-restraint. Self-control is the capacity to manage and control one's way of behaving for accomplishing long haul objectives. It includes settling on decisions that line up with our qualities and desires, even despite prompt delight or outside pressures. Sustaining positive propensities requires a level of self-control, as it includes reliably picking ways of behaving that add to our prosperity.

In the computerized age, the peculiarity of data over-burden represents a test to propensity development. Steady openness to data, notices, and interruptions can thwart our capacity to concentrate and support positive propensities. Creating propensities that relieve data over-burden, for example, computerized detoxes and careful innovation use, is pivotal for keeping a reasonable and purposeful way of life.

The idea of propensity development underscores the unique idea of propensity arrangement. As we develop and advance, our propensities should adjust to line up with our evolving values, objectives, and conditions. Propensity development includes consistently evaluating our propensities, relinquishing those that never again serve us, and developing new ones that help our ongoing direction. It's a course of consistent refinement and transformation chasing self-improvement.

The job of appreciation in supporting positive propensities is a significant part of the propensity development venture. Developing a propensity for appreciation includes consistently recognizing and valuing the positive parts of life. Appreciation fills in as a strong mentality that upgrades prosperity, strength, and generally life fulfillment. Coordinating appreciation rehearses into day to day schedules is a propensity that adds to a positive and hopeful point of view.

The propensity supporting excursion is definitely not a singular undertaking; it includes the interchange of individual endeavors and social impacts. The elements of interpersonal organizations, peer support, and public standards shape the setting inside which propensities are framed. Utilizing the force of social associations, building networks that help positive propensities, and impacting normal practices add to the aggregate exertion of cultivating a culture of prosperity.

The idea of propensity reflection accentuates the significance of consistently evaluating and thinking about our propensities. Propensity reflection includes inspecting the effect of our propensities on different parts of our lives, recognizing regions for development, and praising victories. It's a propensity in itself — one that cultivates mindfulness, learning, and constant enhancement for the propensity sustaining venture.

Chasing positive propensities, the idea of moderation offers an important point of view. Moderation isn't just about cleaning up actual spaces; it stretches out to improving and cleaning up our propensities and responsibilities.

Taking on a moderate outlook includes focusing on fundamental propensities, relinquishing unimportant ones, and making space for deliberate living. Moderation is a focal point through which we can move toward propensity development with lucidity and concentration.

The job of propensities in forming our day to day story is a common subject in the propensity sustaining venture. Our propensities weave the storyline of our lives, impacting the plot and character advancement. Sustaining positive propensities includes making a story that lines up with our qualities and goals. It's about deliberately picking the story we need to tell through our day to day activities and ways of behaving.

In the domain of positive propensities, the idea of stream states is vital. Stream states, portrayed by profound fixation, elevated center, and a feeling of immortality, are ideal states for propensity development. Developing propensities that initiate stream, whether through innovative pursuits, proactive tasks, or care rehearses, upgrades the probability of propensity achievement. Stream states give a rich climate to the consistent combination of positive propensities into our day to day routines.

5.1 Identifying and cultivating positive habits that contribute to inner strength

Recognizing and developing positive propensities that add to inward strength is a groundbreaking excursion that rises above the shallow layers of everyday schedules. It dives into the center of our being, stressing the improvement of propensities that invigorate our flexibility, upgrade our close to home prosperity, and encourage a profound feeling of internal strength. In this investigation, we leave on a journey to figure out the embodiment of internal strength, recognize propensities that support it, and develop a mentality that establishes the groundwork for supported self-awareness.

At the core of the quest for inward strength is the acknowledgment that it goes past simple outside signs of force or perseverance. Internal strength includes close to home versatility, mental guts, and a significant association with one's real self. It includes the capacity to explore difficulties with elegance, keep calm notwithstanding difficulty, and develop a strong soul that endures the back and forth movement of life.

The cycle starts with mindfulness — a foundation of self-improvement. Grasping one's assets, shortcomings, triggers, and close to home examples is the most vital phase in recognizing propensities that add to internal strength. This thoughtful excursion includes a readiness to stand up to and embrace the full range of one's feelings, recognizing weaknesses, and perceiving regions for development. It's a course of stripping back the layers to uncover the genuine self that frames the underpinning of internal strength.

Care arises as a crucial propensity in the journey for inward strength. The act of care includes developing a non-critical familiarity with the current second. A propensity cultivates a profound association with one's viewpoints and feelings, considering a more purposeful reaction to life's difficulties. Through care, people foster the ability to notice their considerations without being consumed by them, cultivating a feeling of internal quiet and lucidity.

Another key propensity that adds to internal strength is the development of a development mentality. Embracing the conviction that difficulties are potential open doors for learning and development enables people to move toward misfortunes with flexibility and assurance. A development mentality is established in the comprehension that capacities can be created, and disappointments are venturing stones toward progress. It supports a positive and versatile way to deal with life's difficulties, cultivating internal strength despite difficulty.

Actual prosperity assumes a significant part in the development of inward strength. Taking on propensities that focus on customary activity, sufficient rest, and a nutritious eating regimen is fundamental. Actual work adds to in general wellbeing as well as significantly affects mental and close to home prosperity. It discharges endorphins, lessens pressure, and improves mental capability — factors that by and large add to a versatile and solid internal identity.

The propensity for self-empathy arises as a directing light on the way to internal strength. Treating oneself with generosity and figuring out, particularly notwithstanding hardships or disappointments, is a groundbreaking propensity. Self-sympathy includes recognizing blemishes without self-judgment, perceiving that enduring is a common human encounter, and stretching out a similar compassion to oneself as one would to a companion. This propensity fabricates a groundwork of confidence and acknowledgment that is fundamental for developing inward strength.

Successful correspondence with oneself as well as other people is a propensity that encourages inward strength. Communicating feelings, necessities, and limits in a reasonable and decisive way adds to a feeling of credibility and strengthening. It includes developing propensities for undivided attention, self-articulation, and solid confidence. This transparent correspondence establishes a steady climate for self-awareness and builds up the inward strength that comes from being consistent with oneself.

The propensity for laying out and seeking after significant objectives is a strong supporter of internal strength. Objectives give guidance, reason, and a feeling of achievement. They act as achievements in the excursion of self-improvement, empowering people to extend past their usual ranges of familiarity and tap into repositories of undiscovered possibility. The quest for objectives encourages a versatile soul that emerges from conquering difficulties and accomplishing achievements en route.

Association with a steady local area is a propensity that essentially adds to inward strength. Developing associations with people who elevate, move, and give a feeling of having a place makes an organization of help. Whether through family, companions, or similar networks, these associations offer profound food, support, and a common feeling of direction. The propensity for sustaining positive connections builds up the internal strength got from a feeling of interconnectedness.

The propensity for persistent learning and personal growth is a powerful power in the excursion toward internal strength. Embracing an outlook that values interest, investigation, and a pledge to long lasting learning encourages scholarly and self-improvement. This propensity includes looking for information, securing new abilities, and being available to different viewpoints. The course of consistent learning enhances the internal identity, giving a feeling of motivation and versatility despite life's intricacies.

Careful using time effectively is a propensity that adds to inward strength by making a feeling of equilibrium and reason. Distinguishing needs, putting forth sensible objectives, and allotting time purposefully forestall sensations of overpower and burnout. This propensity includes standard self-appraisal to guarantee that time is spent on exercises lined up with individual qualities and objectives. Through successful using time effectively, people develop a feeling of command over their lives, supporting inward strength.

Developing the propensity for appreciation is an extraordinary practice that sustains internal strength. Recognizing and valuing the positive parts of life, even amidst difficulties, cultivates an outlook of overflow and flexibility. Appreciation fills in as an offset to cynicism, imparting a feeling of energy and happiness. This propensity includes ordinary reflection on the favors and illustrations in one's day to day existence, making an underpinning of internal strength established in appreciation.

The propensity for versatility includes seeing mishaps not as unrealistic obstructions but rather as any open doors for development. Versatility is the ability to quickly return from misfortune, gaining from difficulties and arising more grounded. A propensity includes reexamining misfortunes, keeping an uplifting perspective, and adjusting to change. Flexibility supports inward strength by ingraining the certainty that one can explore life's vulnerabilities with effortlessness and persistence.

The act of self-reflection is a contemplative propensity that upgrades mindfulness and adds to internal strength. Getting some margin for thoughtfulness includes consistently inspecting contemplations, feelings, and ways of behaving. This propensity permits people to acquire bits of knowledge into their qualities, inspirations, and regions for development. Through self-reflection, people develop a more profound comprehension of themselves, encouraging inward strength through self-information.

Developing the propensity for giving up is a strong supporter of internal strength. Giving up includes delivering connections to results, pardoning oneself as well as other people, and surrendering the weight of past complaints. This propensity opens up mental and profound energy, making space for development and flexibility. An affirmation clutching disdain, responsibility, or unreasonable assumptions obstructs the excursion toward internal strength.

The propensity for embracing isolation is a groundbreaking practice that supports internal strength. Investing energy alone considers self-disclosure, reflection, and a more profound association with one's internal identity. A propensity encourages confidence, freedom, and a feeling of inward harmony. Embracing isolation includes tracking down snapshots of calm reflection, away from outside interruptions, and developing an amicable relationship with oneself.

A foundation propensity in the excursion toward inward strength is the act of taking care of oneself. Taking care of oneself includes focusing on exercises that feed the body, brain, and soul. It includes propensities like sufficient rest, unwinding, inventive articulation, and exercises that give pleasure. Taking care of oneself is a conscious interest in one's prosperity, recognizing that keeping up with internal strength expects consideration regarding physical, profound, and emotional well-being.

The propensity for embracing difficulties with a positive mentality is a groundbreaking practice in the development of inward strength. Rather than review difficulties as unrealistic snags, this propensity includes moving toward them with idealism, versatility, and a confidence in one's capacity to survive. It is a mentality that rethinks challenges as any open doors for development, flexibility, and the reinforcing of internal determination.

The propensity for developing self-restraint is a central component in the excursion toward inward strength. Self-restraint includes settling on purposeful decisions that line up with long haul objectives, even notwithstanding transient allurements. A propensity requires consistency, self control, and a pledge to self-improvement. Through self-restraint, people develop a feeling of dominance over their decisions and activities, supporting inward strength.

The act of defining and keeping up with limits is a propensity that adds to inward strength and prosperity. Limits include characterizing and conveying limits in connections, work, and individual life. This propensity forestalls burnout, encourages solid connections, and guarantees that people focus on their own necessities. Defining and keeping up with limits is a demonstration of self confidence that supports inward strength.

Developing the propensity for pardoning is a groundbreaking practice that sustains inward strength. Pardoning includes delivering hatred and relinquishing the profound weight related with past damages.

A propensity advances close to home recuperating, versatility, and a feeling of internal harmony. Pardoning isn't tied in with overlooking hurtful activities yet about liberating oneself from the shackles of outrage and disdain.

The propensity for embracing change and vulnerability is a unique practice in the development of internal strength. Life is innately erratic, and the capacity to adjust to change is fundamental for strength. This propensity includes fostering an outlook that perspectives change as a characteristic piece of life, a chance for development, and an impetus for self-awareness. Embracing change encourages adaptability, versatility, and internal strength even with vulnerability.

The propensity for rehearsing consideration and sympathy towards oneself as well as other people is an extraordinary practice in the excursion toward internal strength. Developing a caring mentality includes treating oneself with tenderness, stretching out compassion to other people, and cultivating a feeling of interconnectedness. This propensity constructs a groundwork of close to home versatility, advancing a positive inward discourse and building up internal strength.

The act of perception is a strong propensity that adds to inward strength. Representation includes making mental pictures of wanted results, achievement, and the accomplishment of objectives. This propensity upgrades concentration, inspiration, and a positive outlook. By consistently envisioning achievement and positive results, people support a feeling of confidence in their capacities and develop internal strength.

The propensity for offering thanks is a groundbreaking practice that sustains inward strength. Appreciation includes recognizing and valuing the positive parts of life, encouraging a mentality of overflow and energy. This propensity is a strong counteractant to cynicism, ingraining a feeling of happiness and strength. Offering thanks includes routinely thinking about the endowments in one's day to day existence, building up inward strength through appreciation.

Developing the propensity for interest and a hunger for information is a powerful practice in the excursion toward inward strength. An inquisitive outlook includes trying to comprehend, investigate, and gain from the world. This propensity cultivates scholarly development, flexibility, and a feeling of marvel. Through interest, people develop a mentality that values nonstop getting the hang of, supporting internal strength through scholarly and self-awareness.

The propensity for embracing weakness is an extraordinary practice that supports internal strength. Weakness includes the eagerness to show one's bona fide self, share encounters, and interface with others on a more profound level. This propensity cultivates certifiable associations, versatility, and a feeling of genuineness. Embracing weakness is an affirmation that receptiveness and credibility are indispensable to developing internal strength.

The act of keeping a positive inner discourse is a fundamental propensity in the excursion toward internal strength. The manner in which people address themselves inside impacts their convictions, feelings, and activities. Developing a propensity for positive self-talk includes supplanting negative considerations with insisting and engaging explanations. This propensity fabricates a groundwork of self-assurance and supports inward strength.

The propensity for customary reflection and objective reassessment is a powerful practice in the development of internal strength. Life is liquid, and objectives might develop over the long haul. This propensity includes occasionally reconsidering objectives, pondering advancement, and changing course on a case by case basis. Through customary reflection, people keep up with arrangement with their qualities and yearnings, supporting internal strength through purposeful development.

The propensity for looking for snapshots of satisfaction and developing a feeling of energy is an extraordinary practice in the excursion toward internal strength. Life can be testing, and finding snapshots of bliss and liveliness is fundamental for profound prosperity. This propensity includes taking part in exercises that give pleasure, chuckling, and a feeling of softness. Through fun loving nature, people cultivate profound versatility and build up inward strength.

The act of self-articulation through inventiveness is a strong propensity that adds to inward strength. Imagination includes putting oneself out there through different creative or expressive outlets. This propensity cultivates a feeling of genuineness, close to home delivery, and an association with one's internal identity. Through innovative articulation, people develop a more profound comprehension of themselves and build up internal strength.

The propensity for rehearsing care in everyday exercises is a central practice in the development of internal strength. Care includes focusing on the current second without judgment. This propensity improves mindfulness, diminishes pressure, and encourages a feeling of quiet. Through careful living, people develop a mentality of presence and support inward strength in their everyday encounters.

The propensity for embracing isolation and calm reflection is an extraordinary practice that supports inward strength. Isolation gives a space to thoughtfulness, self-revelation, and a more profound association with one's internal identity. This propensity includes finding snapshots of quietude away from outer interruptions. Through isolation, people develop a feeling of internal harmony and support inward strength through thought.

Developing the propensity for rehearsing appreciation in connections is a powerful practice in the excursion toward inward strength. Offering thanks toward others cultivates positive associations, fortifies connections, and builds up a feeling of interconnectedness. This propensity includes recognizing and valuing the commitments of others, building up a positive social climate and adding to inward strength.

The act of defining and regarding individual limits is a central propensity in the excursion toward internal strength. Limits include characterizing and conveying limits in connections, work, and individual life. This propensity cultivates dignity, solid connections, and close to home prosperity. Through the foundation of limits, people build up a feeling of independence and internal strength.

The propensity for rehearsing self-sympathy during testing times is a groundbreaking practice that sustains inward strength. Self-sympathy includes treating oneself with generosity and figuring out, particularly notwithstanding hardships. This propensity encourages close to home strength, self-acknowledgment, and a feeling of internal harmony. Through self-empathy, people build up a positive interior exchange and add to internal strength.

5.2 Practical tips for establishing and maintaining positive routines

Laying out and keeping up with positive schedules is a strong technique for improving efficiency, prosperity, and generally speaking life fulfillment. Schedules give construction, consistency, and a feeling of request in our day to day routines. Whether it's in the domain of wellbeing, work, connections, or self-improvement, positive schedules add to a more deliberate and adjusted way of life. In this investigation, we dig into commonsense tips for laying out as well as supporting positive schedules for long haul achievement.

The most vital phase in laying out certain schedules is to laid out clear and sensible objectives. Characterize what you need to accomplish through your schedules, whether it's better wellbeing, expanded efficiency, upgraded connections, or self-awareness. By having explicit objectives as a top priority, you can tailor your schedules to line up with your yearnings, making them more significant and intentional.

Whenever you've laid out your objectives, separate them into more modest, reasonable assignments. This division makes the objectives more attainable and permits you to integrate them into your everyday schedules without feeling overpowered. For example, in the event that you want to work-out consistently, begin with more limited meetings and steadily increment the power as your routine turns out to be more imbued.

Consistency is the foundation of positive schedules. Pick a set time for your schedules and stick to it as intently as could be expected. Consistency supports the propensity shaping interaction, making it simpler for your psyche and body to adjust. Whether it's awakening simultaneously consistently, booking a devoted work period, or making opportunity for unwinding, consistency fabricates a solid design that turns out to be natural after some time.

To work with consistency, consider integrating your schedules into existing propensities. Partner your new schedules with laid out exercises to make a consistent stream.

For instance, in the event that you plan to foster a morning schedule, connect it to the demonstration of making your bed or having some espresso. This association use existing propensities, making it more straightforward to coordinate and keep up with new sure schedules.

Begin little while presenting new schedules. Start with a couple of sensible propensities to try not to overpower yourself. When these propensities become instilled, progressively present extra components. This gradual methodology permits you to construct positive schedules at a manageable speed, improving the probability of long haul achievement.

Set up a devoted and coordinated space for your schedules. Whether it's a work area, a wellness region, or a tranquil corner for care works on, having an assigned climate helps sign to your cerebrum that now is the right time to participate in a particular daily schedule. A coordinated space likewise diminishes interruptions, establishing a climate helpful for engaged and deliberate way of behaving.

In the domain of positive schedules, focus on taking care of oneself. Dispense time for exercises that sustain your physical, mental, and profound prosperity. Whether it's getting sufficient rest, rehearsing care, or participating in exercises you appreciate, taking care of oneself is central for keeping up with by and large equilibrium and versatility. Integrate taking care of oneself into your everyday schedules to guarantee that it turns into a non-debatable piece of your way of life.

Viable using time productively is a critical part of keeping up with positive schedules. Use devices like schedules, organizers, or efficiency applications to timetable and track your schedules. Set practical time periods for every action, and be aware of how you designate your time over the course of the day. By dealing with your time successfully, you make a construction that upholds the consistency and manageability of positive schedules.

Adaptability is key in adjusting to the powerful idea of life. While schedules give a feeling of request, staying adaptable and open to adjustments is fundamental. Life unavoidably brings unforeseen difficulties and open doors, and being versatile permits you to explore these progressions without crashing your positive schedules. Embrace a mentality that values progress over flawlessness and permits space for changes on a case by case basis.

Responsibility is a strong inspiration in keeping up with positive schedules. Share your objectives and schedules with a companion, relative, or partner who can offer help and consolation. Having somebody to be responsible to improves your obligation to the schedules and makes a feeling of shared liability. Consider cooperating with other people who have comparable objectives to make a strong local area zeroed in on certain propensities.

Think about consistently your schedules and survey their adequacy. Observe what is functioning admirably and what might require change. This self-reflection permits you to tweak your schedules, guaranteeing they stay lined up with your objectives and needs. Be available to trial and error and ready to make changes in view of your developing necessities and conditions.

Integrate components of care into your schedules. Care includes being completely present and participated in the ongoing second. Whether it's during a morning normal, a work task, or an unwinding work on, mixing care into your exercises improves their quality and effect. It likewise cultivates a more profound association with your schedules, making them really satisfying and significant.

Consider making themed days or time blocks in your timetable. This approach permits you to gather comparative assignments, advancing your concentration and proficiency. For example, assign explicit days for centered work, self-awareness, social exercises, and unwinding. Themed days give an unmistakable construction, making it more straightforward to stick to good schedules without feeling dissipated or over-powered.

Praise your triumphs en route. Recognize and compensate yourself for reliably keeping up with positive schedules and accomplishing achievements. Festivities support positive way of behaving and make a positive relationship with your schedules. Whether it's a little treat, a snapshot of reflection, or imparting your accomplishments to other people, perceiving your endeavors adds to a positive mentality and supported inspiration.

Focus on higher expectations when in doubt in your schedules. There's really no need to focus on the number of undertakings you that can pack into a routine however ever about the effect and purposefulness of every action. Center around the nature of your commitment and the positive results instead of attempting to achieve an over the top number of undertakings. This careful methodology upgrades the adequacy and maintainability of your schedules.

In the computerized age, think about utilizing innovation to help your positive schedules. There are various applications and apparatuses intended to help with propensity following, using time effectively, and objective setting. Influence these assets to upgrade your association, keep tabs on your development, and remain persuaded. Nonetheless, be aware of likely interruptions and defined limits to guarantee innovation fills in as a strong device as opposed to a block.

Include your inclinations and interests in your schedules. Whether it's integrating side interests, inventive pursuits, or exercises you truly appreciate, mixing components of delight and energy into your schedules makes them seriously captivating and manageable. This special interaction upgrades your obligation to positive propensities, as you anticipate the satisfying parts of your day to day exercises.

Consistently reevaluate and change your schedules in light of changes in your day to day existence, needs, and objectives. As seasons shift, obligations develop, and individual desires change, your schedules ought to adjust likewise. Be proactive in assessing the importance and viability of your schedules, and alter them to guarantee they stay lined up with your ongoing requirements.

Look for motivation from other people who have effectively settled positive schedules. Gain from their encounters, embrace procedures that impact you, and consolidate components that line up with your objectives. Whether through books, webcasts, or individual discussions, drawing motivation from others gives significant experiences and inspiration to upgrading your own schedules.

Practice self-control in adhering to your schedules, particularly during testing times. While inspiration can change, self-restraint fills in as a solid starting point for keeping up with positive propensities. Develop the capacity to remain focused on your schedules in any event, when confronted with snags or contending needs. Over the long haul, self-restraint turns into an ongoing piece of your mentality, adding to the versatility of your positive schedules.

Make a morning schedule that establishes an uplifting vibe for the afternoon. What you start your day frequently means for its direction. Consolidate exercises that invigorate, propel, and set you up for the day ahead. This could incorporate exercises, for example, work out, care rehearses, objective setting, or a nutritious breakfast. A morning schedule lays out a forward movement that can bring through the remainder of the day.

Lay out limits for your schedules to stay balanced. While consistency is significant, perceiving the requirement for breaks and relaxation is similarly vital. Put forth reasonable lines on the span and power of your schedules, considering times of rest and revival. Offsetting efficiency with snapshots of unwinding adds to the maintainability of positive schedules.

Consider the impact of trained instinct stacking — connecting new propensities with existing ones. This procedure works on the joining of new exercises into your schedules by utilizing the energy of laid out propensities. For instance, on the off chance that you intend to integrate extending into your everyday daily practice, interface it to a current propensity like making your morning espresso. Propensity stacking smoothes out the reception of new ways of behaving, making them more consistent and coordinated.

Develop a positive outlook toward your schedules. Move toward them with energy, seeing them not as errands but rather as purposeful strides toward your objectives. Embrace an outlook that values the worth and effect of positive propensities on your general prosperity. Inspiration improves your inspiration, making it more straightforward to stick to schedules with a feeling of direction and satisfaction.

The act of ordinary activity is a principal part of positive schedules that add to physical and mental prosperity. Whether it's a regular exercise schedule, an energetic walk, or yoga meetings, incorporating active work into your schedules improves energy levels, lessens pressure, and advances generally speaking wellbeing. The propensity for customary activity is a foundation of positive schedules that cultivate comprehensive prosperity.

Consider bunching comparable undertakings together to improve your efficiency. Gathering comparative exercises during explicit time blocks permits you to zero in on each sort of undertaking in turn, limiting setting exchanging and improving productivity. For example, assign explicit periods for email correspondence, innovative work, or authoritative errands. Clustering errands smoothes out your schedules and works on your general work process.

The propensity for ordinary reflection is a groundbreaking practice in keeping up with positive schedules. Put away opportunity to ponder your advancement, difficulties, and changes required in your schedules. This self-reflection encourages mindfulness, permitting you to come to informed conclusions about your propensities and objectives. Consistently survey the arrangement of your schedules with your general goals to guarantee they stay compelling and significant.

Practice appreciation as a piece of your everyday schedules. Integrate snapshots of reflection on the positive parts of your life, offering thanks for both little and critical gifts. The propensity for appreciation develops a positive outlook, improves prosperity, and builds up the deliberateness of your schedules. Appreciation fills in as a strong inspiration, helping you to remember the positive effect your propensities have on your life.

Put resources into nonstop learning and self-awareness as a fundamental piece of your schedules. Devote time to procuring new abilities, understanding books, or taking part in exercises that extend your insight and point of view. The propensity for ceaseless learning adds to scholarly development, versatility, and a feeling of satisfaction. It supports that positive schedules are about upkeep as well as about consistent improvement.

The propensity for defining week by week and month to month objectives supplements your day to day schedules by giving a more extensive viewpoint on your advancement and desires. Set aside some margin to frame explicit targets for the week or month, adjusting them to your overall objectives. This propensity improves your feeling of direction and heading, giving a guide to your schedules and adding to long haul achievement.

Investigate the idea of a computerized detox as a strong practice for keeping up with positive schedules. Consistently detaching from advanced gadgets considers mental restoration, decreased interruptions, and improved center around your schedules. Set assigned times for innovation free exercises, making a space for reflection, inventiveness, and significant commitment with your positive propensities.

Consider making a visual portrayal of your schedules, like an everyday timetable or propensity tracker. Visual guides act as an unmistakable wake up call of your objectives and the means expected to accomplish them. Whether through actual organizers, advanced applications, or straightforward graphs, imagining your schedules upgrades responsibility and inspiration. It gives an unmistakable guide to your everyday exercises and assists you with keeping on track.

Integrate snapshots of unwinding and care into your schedules. Commit time for exercises like profound breathing, reflection, or brief breaks over the course of the day. These snapshots of respite add to pressure decrease, mental lucidity, and by and large prosperity. The propensity for care upgrades your capacity to explore difficulties with levelheadedness and supports the positive effect of schedules on your psychological state.

The act of viable correspondence is a significant propensity for keeping up with positive schedules, particularly in connections and cooperative undertakings. Obviously convey your schedules and assumptions with everyone around you, it are upheld and regarded to guarantee that your positive propensities. Open correspondence encourages understanding and coordinated effort, establishing a climate helpful for the maintainability of your schedules.

Develop the propensity for journaling as an intelligent practice inside your schedules. Routinely write down your viewpoints, encounters, and bits of knowledge connected with your propensities and objectives. Journaling gives a space to self-articulation, lucidity, and self-disclosure. It fills in as an important device for keeping tabs on your development, distinguishing examples, and making informed acclimations to your schedules.

Practice the specialty of expressing no to exercises and responsibilities that don't line up with your needs and objectives. Defining limits is a crucial propensity for safeguarding the significant investment committed to your positive schedules. Amiably yet solidly decline solicitations or commitment that might frustrate your capacity to keep up with consistency in your propensities. Saying no is an engaging practice that builds up your obligation to your prosperity and objectives.

Think about the effect of your current circumstance on your schedules. Make a physical and mental space that upholds your positive propensities. Whether it's getting sorted out your work area, limiting interruptions, or encircling yourself with positive impacts, developing a climate helpful for your objectives improves the manageability of your schedules. Your environmental factors ought to rouse and support the positive ways of behaving you look to lay out.

The propensity for normal social association is fundamental for keeping a decent and satisfying life. Coordinate social exercises into your schedules, whether it's investing energy with family, associating with companions, or participating in local area occasions. Social association adds to profound prosperity, offers help, and adds a feeling of delight to your regular routine. The propensity for supporting connections upgrades the general positive effect of your schedules.

Develop a mentality of appreciation inside your schedules. Routinely express appreciation for the valuable open doors, connections, and encounters in your day to day existence. The propensity for appreciation encourages an inspirational perspective, upgrades your general prosperity, and supports the purposefulness of your schedules. Appreciation fills in as a strong inspiration, helping you to remember the positive effect your propensities have on your life.

As you lay out and keep up with positive schedules, embrace a development mentality. Perceive that progress is a nonstop excursion, and difficulties are open doors for learning and refinement. The propensity for survey difficulties as venturing stones to development cultivates versatility and flexibility. Embrace an outlook that esteems the course of progress, building up the positive effect of your schedules on your self-improvement.

All in all, laying out and keeping up with positive schedules is a dynamic and purposeful excursion that requires responsibility, flexibility, and self-reflection. The tips gave incorporate different parts of prosperity — physical, mental, close to home, and social. By defining clear objectives, cultivating consistency, rehearsing taking care of oneself, and staying open to changes, you make an establishment for supported positive propensities. The excursion isn't about flawlessness however about progress, development, and the nonstop refinement of schedules that add to an intentional and satisfying life.

5.3 The science behind the impact of habits on mental and emotional well-being

The many-sided transaction among propensities and mental and profound prosperity is a subject well established in logical request. As scientists dive into the intricacies of the human psyche, they reveal an abundance of proof supporting the significant effect of propensities on psychological wellness, close to home flexibility, and in general prosperity. This investigation discloses the logical underpinnings of how propensities shape brain connections, impact mind science, and add to the complicated woven artwork of our psychological and profound lives.

At the brain level, propensities make a permanent imprint on the cerebrum's engineering. The course of propensity arrangement includes the creation and support of brain processes — associations between neurons that fortify with reiteration. As propensities become instilled, these brain processes set, making the related ways of behaving more programmed and proficient. Brain adaptability, the mind's capacity to adjust and revamp itself, is a key component that highlights the flexibility of these brain associations.

The basal ganglia, a district profound inside the cerebrum, assumes a significant part in propensity development. This design is engaged with the coordination of engine developments, as well as the turn of events and execution of schedules.

As propensities become everyday practice, the basal ganglia expects a focal job in their execution, opening up higher cerebrum capabilities for additional complex mental undertakings. This brain proficiency is a demonstration of the cerebrum's versatile limit, permitting it to smooth out routine ways of behaving to preserve mental assets.

Dopamine, a synapse frequently connected with delight and prize, is a central member in the study of propensity development. The mind discharges dopamine in light of remunerating improvements, building up the association between a particular way of behaving and the positive result related with it. This neurochemical reward framework is a main thrust behind the support of propensities. As people experience the beneficial outcomes of a propensity, whether it's the fulfillment of finishing a responsibility or the delight in a pleasurable action, the mind discharges dopamine, reinforcing the brain connections related with that way of behaving.

On the other hand, propensities likewise impact the mind's pressure reaction through the connection with the nerve center pituitary-adrenal (HPA) hub. Ongoing pressure, frequently exacerbated by bad things to do or the shortfall of positive ones, can prompt dysregulation in the HPA hub, bringing about delayed rise of pressure chemicals like cortisol. This dysregulation adds to an elevated condition of excitement, influencing mental and close to home prosperity. Positive propensities, then again, can go about as supports, relieving the impacts of weight on the HPA hub and advancing a more adjusted pressure reaction.

The prefrontal cortex, answerable for leader works, for example, navigation, drive control, and objective setting, is very familiar in the guideline of propensities. It applies hierarchical command over the basal ganglia, tweaking the commencement and execution of constant ways of behaving. This complicated dance between the prefrontal cortex and the basal ganglia is pivotal for the guideline of propensities, taking into consideration a harmony between programmed, routine ways of behaving and all the more intellectually requesting errands.

With regards to mental and close to home prosperity, the effect of propensities stretches out past the domain of brain processes. Constant ways of behaving add to the development of mental examples and profound reactions. The mental conduct viewpoint sets that constant considerations and ways of behaving impact feelings and, equally, profound states shape ongoing reactions. For instance, an individual who reliably participates in pessimistic self-talk might foster propensities for cynicism, impacting their profound prosperity over the long run.

Propensities likewise assume a critical part in molding the mind's default mode organization (DMN), an organization of cerebrum districts dynamic during rest and self-referential reasoning. The DMN is ensnared in cycles, for example, fantasizing, mind-meandering, and contemplation. Positive propensities, especially those that include care and self-reflection, can add to a more adjusted and versatile DMN, cultivating a condition of mental prosperity. Alternately, negative propensities that sustain rumination and unnecessary self-analysis might add to dysregulation in the DMN, worsening psychological wellness challenges.

The effect of propensities on mental and close to home prosperity is additionally highlighted by their impact on synapses, for example, serotonin and gamma-aminobutyric corrosive (GABA). Serotonin, frequently alluded to as the "vibe great" synapse, assumes a urgent part in mind-set guideline. Propensities that advance positive social associations, actual work, and taking care of oneself add to the delivery and guideline of serotonin, encouraging close to home prosperity. GABA, an inhibitory synapse, is related with unwinding and stress decrease. Propensities, for example, care rehearses and satisfactory rest decidedly impact GABA levels, advancing a feeling of quiet and profound strength.

The idea of "close to home granularity" features the job of propensities in molding the explicitness and subtlety of profound encounters. Close to home granularity alludes to the capacity to recognize, separate, and express a large number of feelings. Positive propensities, particularly those that include profound articulation and mindfulness, add to upgraded close to home granularity. On the other hand, constant concealment of feelings or commitment to maladaptive survival techniques might lessen close to home granularity, influencing emotional wellness.

The bidirectional connection among propensities and mental and profound prosperity is apparent with regards to fixation. Substance use problems, described by impulsive medication chasing and use regardless of hurtful results, embody the strong effect of adjustment on the mind's award framework. Routine medication use prompts neuroadaptations in the mind, capturing the prize hardware and adding to a pattern of compulsion. The negative impacts of habit-forming propensities on mental and close to home prosperity highlight the significant impact of propensities on brain processes and conduct.

Positive propensities, notwithstanding, can act as integral assets in compulsion recuperation. The development of option, solid propensities can assist with overhauling brain connections, furnishing people with valuable survival strategies and a feeling of direction. The brain adaptability of the mind takes into account the steady supplanting of maladaptive propensities with positive ones, supporting long haul recuperation and mental prosperity.

The study of propensities likewise reveals insight into the job of propensities in the turn of events and support of emotional wellness issues. Propensities that add to a sound way of life, like standard activity, nutritious eating, and adequate rest, are related with a lower hazard of emotional well-being issues. These propensities impact synapse equilibrium, brain adaptability, and stress flexibility, making an establishment for mental prosperity.

Then again, negative propensities, like inactive way of behaving, unfortunate dietary decisions, and sporadic rest designs, are connected to an expanded gamble of psychological wellness challenges.

The effect of these propensities on foundational irritation, synapse awkwardness, and hormonal guideline adds to the weakness to conditions like sorrow and tension. Understanding the science behind these affiliations features the significance of developing positive propensities for emotional wellness advancement and intercession.

Care rehearses, established in the development of present-second mindfulness, epitomize the neuroscientific underpinnings of positive propensities. Care draws in mind districts related with consideration, mindfulness, and close to home guideline. Customary care practice has been displayed to prompt underlying and utilitarian changes in the cerebrum, especially in areas ensnared in pressure reaction and feeling guideline. The study of care highlights its true capacity as a groundbreaking propensity for mental and profound prosperity.

Rest, a principal part of day to day existence, is unpredictably connected to mental and close to home prosperity through the study of circadian rhythms and rest engineering. Propensities that focus on steady rest designs and establish a favorable rest climate add to ideal circadian guideline. The effect of rest on synapse balance, memory union, and profound handling features the bidirectional connection between rest propensities and psychological wellness.

Social association, a strong determinant of mental and profound prosperity, is impacted by propensities for relational commitment. Positive social propensities, like customary mingling, empathic correspondence, and thoughtful gestures, add to the arrival of oxytocin, a chemical related with social holding and trust. These propensities upgrade social help, encourage a feeling of having a place, and decidedly impact emotional wellness.

The effect of propensities on mental and profound prosperity isn't bound to individual way of behaving; it reaches out to the aggregate level. Social and social propensities shape the emotional well-being scene of networks and social orders. Social standards, cultural assumptions, and mutual propensities impact the predominance and shame related with psychological wellness issues. Understanding the cultural setting of propensities gives experiences into the more extensive determinants of mental and profound prosperity.

The logical investigation of propensities and their effect on mental and profound prosperity accentuates the dynamic and interconnected nature of these cycles. Brain pliancy, synapse guideline, mental examples, and profound reactions by and large add to the multifaceted dance among propensities and psychological wellness. This understanding offers an establishment for the improvement of intercessions and systems that bridle the versatile limit of the cerebrum to develop.

Chapter 6

Connecting with Purpose

Interfacing with design is a significant excursion that rises above the conventional texture of our lives. It includes adjusting our activities, goals, and values with a more profound feeling of importance and importance. This investigation dives into the diverse elements of associating with reason, drawing bits of knowledge from brain research, theory, and self-improvement. From understanding the quintessence of direction to useful procedures for its revelation and mix, this excursion is an odyssey into the actual center of human life.

At its pith, object is the main thrust that moves people toward a significant and satisfying life. The compass guides choices, activities, and the quest for objectives. Mentally, intention is unpredictably connected to a feeling of personality and self-revelation. It gives a structure to figuring out one's position on the planet and the effect of individual commitments. The mission for object is woven into the texture of the human experience, and its interest turns into a groundbreaking excursion of self-acknowledgment.

The prestigious clinician Viktor Frankl, in his fundamental work "Man's Quest for Importance," investigates the meaning of direction despite misfortune. In view of his encounters as a Holocaust survivor, Frankl places that tracking down importance throughout everyday life, even in the most difficult conditions, is a basic human need. He presents the idea of logotherapy, a psychotherapeutic methodology focused on the quest for significance as a main impetus for prosperity. Frankl's work highlights the versatility that arises when people interface with a feeling of direction, even in the midst of significant torment.

Logically, reason has been a focal topic in existentialist idea. Existential savants like Jean-Paul Sartre and Albert Camus wrestle with the innate opportunity and obligation that accompany making one's motivation. Sartre broadly states, "Man is sentenced to be free; on the grounds that once tossed into the world, he is answerable for all that he does." This existential point of view underscores the independence and organization people have in deeply shaping their lives through deliberate decisions.

The quest for intention is profoundly interwoven with the idea of eudaimonia, a term from old Greek way of thinking that implies human prospering or the most elevated human great. Aristotle, a noticeable defender of eudaimonia, sets that living as per one's real essence and realizing one's expected prompts an existence of excellence and prosperity. According to an Aristotelian point of view, reason rises out of the bona fide articulation of individual abilities, ethics, and the quest for greatness.

Interfacing with reason includes a course of self-disclosure, wherein people investigate their qualities, interests, and exceptional commitments to the world. This reflective excursion requires a profound comprehension of one's center convictions, the exercises that give pleasure and satisfaction, and the effect one tries to make. Through self-reflection and care, people gain lucidity about their motivation and create a guide for adjusting their lives to this significant internal compass.

Values assume a crucial part in the journey for reason. They address the key convictions and rules that guide independent direction and conduct. Recognizing and focusing on fundamental beliefs is an essential move toward interfacing with reason. This cycle includes considering the main thing, the rules that resound profoundly, and the sort of individual one tries to be. Articulating values makes a compass that assists people with exploring life's intricacies and settle on decisions lined up with their legitimate selves.

Interests and interests are powerful signs of direction. Taking part in exercises that give pleasure, energy, and a feeling of satisfaction frequently divulges parts of one's motivation. Investigating leisure activities, imaginative pursuits, and areas of certified revenue permits people to take advantage of their inborn inspiration and find aspects of their motivation. Enthusiastic commitment encourages a profound association with one's internal identity, giving significant insights on the way to deliberate living.

Significant associations with others contribute fundamentally to the feeling of direction. Building connections, encouraging local area, and adding to the prosperity of others are aspects of direction that reach out past individual satisfaction. Social analyst Roy Baumeister's exploration on the requirement for belongingness accentuates the significant effect of significant connections on generally speaking prosperity. Thoughtful gestures, sympathy, and coordinated effort make a feeling of interconnected reason, where individual desires line up with the aggregate great.

The quest for design is frequently interlaced with the idea of calling — a business or a feeling of being attracted to a specific life way. Clinician William Damon investigates the possibility of the "deliberate self" and the groundbreaking force of a calling. A calling gives an internal compass that goes past private accomplishment to add to a more prominent great. Whether it's a calling to a particular calling, a reason, or a lifestyle, the affirmation and quest for a calling inject existence with a more profound feeling of significance.

The Japanese idea of "ikigai" exemplifies the crossing point of what one loves, what one is great at, what the world requirements, and what one can be paid for. Ikigai addresses the perfect balance where enthusiasm, business, calling, and mission combine. Finding one's ikigai is a strong structure for interfacing with reason, as it exemplifies the all encompassing elements of a satisfying life. This idea urges people to look for the amicable mix of different perspectives to have an existence wealthy in reason and fulfillment.

Analyst Ditty Dweck's work on outlook further enlightens the association between one's convictions and the quest for reason. A development mentality, described by the conviction that capacities can be created through devotion and difficult work, cultivates a more versatile way to deal with difficulties. Embracing a development outlook is helpful for the quest for reason, as it empowers strength, learning, and an eagerness to investigate new roads on the excursion to self-revelation.

Developing strength is basic to the excursion of interfacing with reason. Strength, the capacity to return from mishaps and misfortune, is a powerful quality that supports people on their intentional way. Embracing difficulties as any open doors for development, rethinking disappointments as growth opportunities, and keeping a feeling of positive thinking add to the flexibility expected to explore the intricacies of deliberate living.

Care rehearses, established in the development of present-second mindfulness, are important apparatuses for associating with reason. Care improves mindfulness, diminishes mental mess, and encourages a more profound comprehension of one's qualities and goals. By rehearsing care, people make space for reflection, lucidity, and a more purposeful way to deal with life. Care fills in as a pondering anchor that upholds the excursion of deliberate living.

The effect of direction on mental and close to home prosperity is a point of convergence of examination in sure brain science. Studies have shown that people with areas of strength for an of direction experience more elevated levels of life fulfillment, lower levels of pressure, and more noteworthy mental prosperity. Intentional living is related with improved versatility, better close to home guideline, and an inspirational perspective on life. The pursuit and fulfillment of direction add to a more significant and satisfying presence.

Clinician Abraham Maslow, in his order of necessities, places self-completion at the zenith — a level where people understand their maximum capacity and take a stab at self-awareness and satisfaction. Interfacing with reason adjusts intimately with the quest for self-completion, as it includes the acknowledgment of one's remarkable capacities, values, and desires. Self-realization through intentional living is an extraordinary excursion that rises above essential requirements and adds to the comprehensive thriving of the person.

The positive effect of direction on actual wellbeing is an arising area of examination. Studies recommend that people with major areas of strength for an of direction might encounter better cardiovascular wellbeing, worked on safe capability, and expanded life span. Intentional living is related with better way of life decisions, like normal activity, nutritious eating, and better rest designs. The brain body association highlights the integrative idea of direction in affecting generally speaking prosperity.

The advantages of direction reach out to the work environment, where people who view as importance and importance in their work report higher work fulfillment and commitment. The arrangement of individual qualities with proficient objectives adds to a feeling of satisfaction and inspiration. Associations that encourage a feeling of direction among representatives frequently experience expanded efficiency, innovativeness, and a good hierarchical culture. Reason driven work makes a harmonious connection between individual satisfaction and aggregate achievement.

With regards to training, the reconciliation of deliberate learning upgrades understudy commitment and scholastic achievement. At the point when instructive encounters line up with understudies' inclinations, values, and yearnings, the growing experience turns out to be more significant and groundbreaking. Teachers assume a urgent part in directing understudies toward self-disclosure, empowering investigation of interests, and encouraging a feeling of direction that stretches out past the homeroom.

6.1 Exploring the significance of purpose in finding inner strength

Investigating the meaning of direction in finding inward strength discloses a significant exchange between a feeling of importance, flexibility, and individual grit. Reason, frequently viewed as the main thrust that provides guidance to life, goes past simple objectives and accomplishments; it turns into an anchor that supports people through difficulties and engages them to explore the intricacies of presence. This investigation dives into the mental, close to home, and existential elements of how reason fills in as an impetus for creating internal strength.

At the mental level, reason assumes a pivotal part in molding one's personality and giving a system to figuring out the self comparable to the world. Clinicians and researchers have long investigated the association between a feeling of direction and mental prosperity. Erik Erikson, a trailblazer in formative brain research, presented the idea of personality versus job disarray, underlining the significance of framing a cognizant identity. Reason, as a vital part of personality, adds to a steady and versatile self-idea.

The mental meaning of direction is exemplified in Frankl's logotherapy, which sets that the essential human drive is the quest for significance. Frankl, a Holocaust survivor and specialist, noticed the groundbreaking force of direction even with significant misery. His encounters drove him to presume that people who find importance in their lives are better prepared to get through difficulties and keep a feeling of internal strength. Reason turns into a mental anchor that gives strength notwithstanding difficulty.

Besides, positive brain research, a field that spotlights on human prospering and prosperity, highlights the significance of direction as a vital component of a satisfying life. Concentrates on inside the positive brain research system uncover that people with major areas of strength for an of direction experience more significant levels of life fulfillment, a more noteworthy feeling of importance, and expanded generally speaking prosperity.

The mental advantages of direction stretch out to improved profound guideline, lower levels of pressure, and an inspirational perspective on life.

In the domain of profound prosperity, reason fills in as a wellspring of natural inspiration and satisfaction. Feelings, frequently thought to be the compass of human experience, are significantly impacted by the arrangement of activities with a feeling of direction. At the point when people participate in exercises that reverberate with their qualities and add to a more prominent great, they experience a profound feeling of fulfillment and delight. This close to home reverberation builds up internal strength by encouraging a positive profound express that goes about as a support against the difficulties of life.

The quest for reason includes an investigation of interests, interests, and the one of a kind commitments people can make to the world. At the point when people interface with exercises that give them certified pleasure and satisfaction, they tap into a wellspring of positive feelings. The profound meaning of direction is obvious in the delight gotten from imaginative pursuits, the fulfillment of adding to others' prosperity, and the satisfaction that comes from living truly. These positive feelings, interweaved with reason, become a supply of internal strength that supports people through the ups and downs of life.

Moreover, reason gives a significant setting to handling and exploring feelings, incorporating those related with difficulty and vulnerability. At the point when people face difficulties or mishaps, a feeling of direction offers a system for grasping the more extensive meaning of these encounters. The profound flexibility got from reason empowers people to adapt to hardships, track down importance in misfortune, and keep a feeling of inward strength even despite close to home choppiness.

Existentially, reason turns into an essential anchor in the journey for a significant life. Existential logicians, like Jean-Paul Sartre and Albert Camus, wrestled with inquiries of significance and the human condition. Sartre's idea of "dishonesty" features the aversion of legitimate living when people disregard the obligation of making their own motivation. Conversely, reason driven living lines up with existential standards by stressing individual organization, decision, and the formation of a daily existence permeated with significance.

The existential meaning of direction is exemplified in the idea of "credibility." Living really includes adjusting one's activities and decisions to a self-determined feeling of direction, liberated from cultural assumptions or outside pressures. Existential realness isn't a landing in a decent objective yet a continuous course of self-disclosure and deliberate living. Embracing one's bona fide reason turns into an extraordinary excursion that encourages inward strength by lining up with the center of one's being.

Existential brain science, as evolved by Viktor Frankl, stresses the quest for significance as a principal part of the human experience. Frankl's perceptions in death camps drove him to presume that people who tracked down significance, whether in little thoughtful gestures or bigger existential objects, were stronger despite anguish. Reason, in an existential setting, turns into a reference point that enlightens the way to internal strength by giving a system to rising above difficulty through the quest for importance.

The existential meaning of direction additionally connects with the idea of "unfaltering addressing," where people effectively draw in with the existential inquiries of life. Investigating inquiries concerning reason, presence, and the idea of one's process cultivates a more profound association with inward strength. The course of steadfast addressing urges people to face the vulnerabilities of existence with boldness and interest, adding to the improvement of a strong and reason driven outlook.

Additionally, the connection among reason and flexibility is clear in research on post-awful development. People who face injury or misfortune might encounter significant mental development, prompting expanded strength and a more profound feeling of direction. This peculiarity, recorded in the repercussions of different life challenges, highlights the extraordinary capability of direction in developing internal strength. The capacity to get significance from difficulty and influence it for self-improvement mirrors the flexibility that reason imparts.

Essentially, finding and living with reason includes an intentional and continuous course of self-investigation. The viable components of interfacing with reason incorporate distinguishing fundamental beliefs, investigating interests, putting forth significant objectives, and adjusting everyday activities to a feeling of direction. Reasonable procedures for finding reason incorporate thoughtful practices, objective setting, and taking part in exercises that line up with one's qualities and interests.

Contemplation, as a down to earth device for self-revelation, includes considering individual qualities, interests, and desires. Normal reflection makes a space for people to acquire clearness about what makes the biggest difference to them, preparing for the recognizable proof of a reason that reverberates truly. Journaling, contemplation, and care rehearses are commonsense strategies that work with reflection and upgrade mindfulness in the excursion toward reason.

Defining significant objectives is one more reasonable procedure for interfacing with reason. Reason driven objectives give an unmistakable course to people to channel their energy and endeavors. These objectives line up with one's qualities and desires, making a feeling of intentional force. Whether present moment or long haul, reason driven objectives act as venturing stones that add to the advancement of inward strength through deliberate activity and progress.

Participating in exercises that line up with individual qualities and interests is a commonsense pathway to deliberate living. Whether through side interests, chipping in, or proficient pursuits, people can mix reason into their day to day routines by effectively taking part in exercises that reverberate with their bona fide selves. These reason driven exercises add to a feeling of satisfaction and versatility, supporting internal strength through the arrangement of activities with reason.

Moreover, mentorship and direction assume functional parts in the excursion of associating with reason. Looking for the insight and experiences of tutors, good examples, or people who have strolled comparable ways can give important direction. Tutors can offer point of view, share encounters, and offer help in exploring the difficulties of direction revelation. Their direction turns into a useful asset for people looking to foster internal strength through deliberate living.

The pragmatic parts of associating with reason reach out to the work environment and authoritative settings. Associations that cultivate a feeling of direction among representatives frequently experience expanded efficiency, work fulfillment, and a good hierarchical culture. Pioneers can assume a functional part in establishing reason driven workplaces by adjusting hierarchical qualities to individual desires and giving roads to representatives to interface with a bigger mission.

Besides, the useful ramifications of direction are clear in the field of training. Teachers can work with reason investigation by establishing learning conditions that urge understudies to investigate their interests, values, and expected commitments to the world. Incorporating reason driven training includes pragmatic systems, for example, project-based learning, mentorship projects, and educational plans that stress the association between scholastic pursuits and certifiable effect.

The job of local area and social association in functional reason disclosure is essential. Drawing in with similar people, partaking in local area exercises, and building social associations add to the down to earth components.

6.2 Exercises to help readers clarify and align with their life's purpose

Leaving on the excursion to explain and line up with life's motivation is an extraordinary interaction that requires thoughtfulness, self-disclosure, and deliberate activity. Participating in deliberate activities can act as a compass, directing people toward a more profound comprehension of their qualities, interests, and goals. These activities offer pragmatic devices to unwind the layers of mindfulness and enlighten the way toward a more intentional life. Whether investigating basic beliefs, distinguishing interests, defining significant objectives, or making an individual statement of purpose, these activities make a guide for people to interface with their exceptional reason.

Values Investigation:

The groundwork of direction frequently lays on a strong comprehension of individual qualities. Start by considering the qualities that resound profoundly with you. What standards guide your choices and activities? Make a rundown of your guiding principle, and afterward focus on them in light of their importance. This exercise permits you to explain the rules that structure the bedrock of your feeling of direction.

Practice Steps:

Make a rundown of values that vibe essential to you (e.g., trustworthiness, sympathy, imagination).

Focus on these qualities from most to least significant.

Ponder why each worth holds importance for you.

Consider how these qualities manifest in your everyday existence.

By getting it and focusing on your qualities, you lay the basis for adjusting your activities to what makes the biggest difference to you.

Energy Investigation:

Uncovering your interests is a crucial stage in the excursion toward reason. What exercises give you pleasure and satisfaction? Think about the minutes when you feel generally invigorated and locked in. This exercise urges you to investigate your inclinations, side interests, and the exercises that resound with your valid self.

Practice Steps:

Make a rundown of exercises that you really appreciate.

Consider when you feel generally energetic and satisfied.

Distinguish normal topics or examples in these exercises.

Consider how you can incorporate a greater amount of these enthusiasm driven exercises into your life.

Investigating your interests gives significant experiences into the exercises that line up with your credible self, directing you toward deliberate living.

Objective Setting with Reason:

Reason traveled objectives go about as achievements on your excursion toward a significant life. Put forth objectives that line up with your qualities and interests, making a guide for individual and expert development. This exercise includes distinguishing present moment and long haul objectives that mirror your goals and add to your feeling of direction.

Practice Steps:

Characterize explicit present moment and long haul objectives.

Guarantee that every objective lines up with your qualities and interests.

Separate bigger objectives into noteworthy stages.

Lay out a course of events for accomplishing these objectives.

Objective setting with reason changes yearnings into substantial, feasible advances, encouraging an internal compass and achievement.

Life Vision Board:

Representation is a useful asset for showing your desires. Make a day to day existence vision board that outwardly addresses your ideal life and the objectives you wish to accomplish. This exercise takes advantage of the inventive part of your brain, making your desires more unmistakable and convincing.

Practice Steps:

Accumulate magazines, pictures, and statements that reverberate with your objectives and values.

Make a montage on a board or carefully that addresses your optimal life.

Place the vision board in a noticeable area.

Consistently return to and update the board as your objectives advance.

The existence vision board fills in as a day to day sign of your motivation, mooring your desires in the visual portrayal of your optimal life.

Ikigai Investigation:

The Japanese idea of Ikigai addresses the convergence of what you love, what you are great at, what the world requirements, and what you can be paid for. This exercise guides you through the most common way of finding your Ikigai, a strong structure for interfacing with your motivation.

Practice Steps:

Make four records: What you love, What you are great at, What the world necessities, and What you can be paid for.

Investigate the covers between these rundowns to distinguish possible areas of direction.

Think about how you can incorporate these components into your day to day existence.

Utilize this blend to illuminate your choices and activities.

Ikigai gives an all encompassing viewpoint, assisting you with distinguishing the intermingling of energy, livelihood, mission, and calling.

Individual Statement of purpose:

Making an individual statement of purpose is a strong practice in refining your motivation into a succinct and significant assertion. This exercise includes articulating your qualities, interests, and yearnings such that fills in as a directing light for your life's process.

Practice Steps:

Consider your qualities, interests, and long haul objectives.

Compose a draft statement of purpose that epitomizes your feeling of direction.

Alter and refine the assertion until it compactly catches your substance.

Consistently return to and change your statement of purpose as you advance.

A very much created statement of purpose turns into a compass, giving clearness and concentration as you explore the different features of your life.

Account Reflection:

Pondering your life's account includes investigating the narratives and encounters that have molded you. This exercise urges you to distinguish urgent minutes, difficulties, and accomplishments, knowing examples that add to your feeling of direction.

Practice Steps:

Diary about critical life altering situations, both positive and testing.Recognize normal topics or repeating themes in these encounters.

Consider the illustrations advanced and how they add to your self-improvement.

Consider how your story lines up with your advancing feeling of direction.

Story reflection gives a more profound comprehension of your excursion, enlightening the strings that weave your novel story of direction.

Care and Reason:

Coordinating care rehearses into your day to day schedule upgrades mindfulness and presence, key components in the excursion toward reason. This exercise includes consolidating care strategies to develop a condition of mindfulness and purposefulness.

Practice Steps:

Begin with short care rehearses, like careful breathing or contemplation.

Incorporate care into routine exercises, encouraging a feeling of presence.

Consider how care improves your familiarity with values and reason.

Investigate care rehearses that line up with your feeling of direction.

Care fills in as an establishing work on, encouraging a more profound association with your qualities and directing you toward deliberate living.

Commitment Diary:

Following your commitments to other people and the world is an intelligent activity that underlines the effect of your activities. This exercise includes keeping a commitment diary to report snapshots of thoughtfulness, backing, and positive impact.

Practice Steps:

Keep a diary to record examples where you had a beneficial outcome.

Think about the sentiments related with adding to others' prosperity.

Recognize designs in the ways you add to your local area or the world.

Utilize this diary as a wellspring of motivation and a sign of your ability to have an effect.

The commitment diary builds up the association among reason and having a significant effect on the existences of others.

Input and Reflection Circle:

Taking part in a consistent criticism and reflection circle includes looking for input from confided in companions, guides, or associates. This exercise urges you to assemble points of view on your assets, interests, and areas of development, adding to progressing self-revelation.

Practice Steps:

Request input from people who realize you well.

Request bits of knowledge on your assets, regions for advancement, and noticed interests.

Ponder the input and consider how it lines up with your self-insight.

Utilize this data to refine how you might interpret your one of a kind characteristics and reason.

The input and reflection circle gives outer points of view that supplement your interior investigation, adding to a more comprehensive comprehension of your motivation.

6.3 Individuals who discovered their inner strength through a sense of purpose

The tales of people who have found their inward strength through a significant feeling of direction act as moving stories that enlighten the groundbreaking force of direction in the human experience. These accounts, woven through the texture of different lives, uncover the strength, assurance, and mettle that emerge when people interface with a more profound significance and course. From conquering individual difficulties to making huge commitments to the world, these people epitomize the significant effect of direction in opening inward strength.

One such rousing story is that of Malala Yousafzai, a Pakistani extremist for female schooling and the most youthful ever Nobel Prize laureate. Malala found her inward strength through her relentless obligation to pushing for young ladies' schooling despite affliction. Experiencing childhood in the Smack Valley of Pakistan, Malala saw the Taliban's rising impact and their endeavors to confine young ladies' admittance to training. In 2012, she endure a designated death endeavor by the Taliban, supporting perilous wounds.

Malala's feeling of direction became obvious as she kept on supporting schooling for young ladies, even in the consequence of the assault. Her flexibility and assurance to seek after her objective, undaunted by private risk, displayed the internal strength that emerges when one lines up with a reason bigger than oneself. Malala's responsibility prompted the foundation of the Malala Asset, a non-benefit association pushing for young ladies' schooling universally. Through her story, Malala represents how reason can turn into a main thrust that changes individual misfortune into an impetus for positive change.

Another convincing model is the tale of Mahatma Gandhi, a head of the Indian autonomy development who utilized peaceful common noncompliance to lead his country to independence from English rule.

Gandhi's internal strength was well established in his obligation to standards of truth, peacefulness, and administration to mankind. His feeling of direction was fashioned through a profound otherworldly and philosophical excursion, driving him to advocate for equity, equity, and opportunity.

Gandhi's way was set apart by various difficulties, including detainment, fasting, and confronting savagery. However, his faithful obligation to his standards and his vision of a free and impartial India energized his versatility. His way of thinking of Satyagraha, meaning the emphasis on truth and the quest for moral power, turned into a directing light for those looking for opportunity and equity.

Gandhi's inward strength, drawn from his significant feeling of direction, motivated millions and keeps on impacting developments for equity and basic liberties around the world. His life epitomizes how reason might not just sustain a singular's purpose at any point yet additionally become a signal for cultural change.

In the domain of science and development, the narrative of Marie Curie grandstands how a feeling of direction can drive people to push the limits of information. Marie Curie, a spearheading physicist and scientific expert, made earth shattering commitments to the comprehension of radioactivity and the improvement of X-beam innovation. Her revelations procured her two Nobel Prizes, making her the primary lady to get this distinction in two different logical fields.

Marie Curie's feeling of direction was established in her tenacious quest for logical information and her longing to add to humankind's prosperity. Notwithstanding confronting orientation predisposition in the male-ruled academic local area, she drove forward in her examination, driven by a promise to disentangle the secrets of the regular world. Her momentous work progressed science as well as established the groundwork for clinical headways in the finding and treatment of sicknesses.

Curie's life shows how a profound feeling of direction can fuel persistence even with deterrents, prompting groundbreaking commitments that stretch out a long ways past individual achievements. Her inheritance keeps on motivating hopeful researchers and supporters for orientation uniformity in science.

The tale of Nelson Mandela, the counter politically-sanctioned racial segregation progressive and previous leader of South Africa, is one more remarkable demonstration of the groundbreaking effect of direction on inward strength. Mandela's motivation was pull in the journey for equity, equity, and the destroying of the harsh arrangement of politically-sanctioned racial segregation. His obligation to these standards prompted his detainment for quite a long time.

During his detainment, Mandela's feeling of direction stayed whole. He involved his time in jail to additional his schooling, participate in political conversations with individual detainees, and keep an undaunted obligation to the beliefs of a free and vote based South Africa. Upon his delivery in 1990, Mandela kept on driving the battle against politically-sanctioned racial segregation, at last turning into the nation's most memorable dark president in 1994.

Mandela's capacity to pardon and accommodate with the people who had mistreated him shown the groundbreaking force of direction in developing inward strength. His administration during a vital period in South Africa's set of experiences exhibited the versatility that arises when an individual is lined up with a more noble end goal. Mandela's inheritance fills in as a worldwide image of the victory of equity, pardoning, and compromise over mistreatment and contempt.

In the realm of writing, the tale of Viktor Frankl, an Austrian nervous system specialist and therapist, gives significant bits of knowledge into the human ability to track down internal strength through a feeling of direction. Frankl's life was significantly molded by his encounters as a Holocaust survivor. Imprisoned in death camps during The Second Great War, Frankl saw the outrageous profundities of human affliction and the dehumanizing impacts of severity.

Frankl's feeling of direction arose out of his assurance to track down importance even amidst impossible misery. He saw that the individuals who endure the camps frequently had a feeling of direction that headed past their own conditions. In his original work, "Man's Quest for Importance," Frankl stated, "Everything can be taken from a man however a certain something: the remainder of the human opportunities — to pick one's disposition in some random situation, to pick one's direction."

Frankl's existential way of thinking, known as logotherapy, fixates on the possibility that finding importance is fundamental for human prosperity. His own endurance notwithstanding outrageous misfortune epitomizes the versatility that can be drawn from a profound feeling of direction. Frankl's commitments to brain research and his accentuation on the quest for importance as a major human drive keep on impacting the fields of existential brain research and psychotherapy.

These stories by and large show the different manners by which people have found their internal strength through a significant feeling of direction. Whether pushing for equity, progressing logical information, defeating individual misfortune, or adding to cultural change, these people represent the extraordinary influence of direction in shaping lives and leaving persevering through heritages.

Significantly, these accounts offer important illustrations for those on their own excursion of self-disclosure and reason. They highlight the possibility that design isn't only an elevated ideal however a powerful power that can direct people through difficulties, rouse flexibility, and lead to significant commitments to the world.

The stories of Malala Yousafzai, Mahatma Gandhi, Marie Curie, Nelson Mandela, and Viktor Frankl motivate people to consider their own qualities, interests, and desires, welcoming them to interface with a reason that rises above private limits.

As people explore the intricacies of life, these accounts advise them that finding internal strength through design is definitely not a one-time accomplishment however a continuous excursion. It includes ceaseless self-reflection, arrangement with basic beliefs, and a pledge to having a beneficial outcome on the world. The stories of these exceptional people act as encouraging signs, empowering others to leave on their own missions for reason, flexibility, and a day to day existence profoundly implanted with significance.

The mission for internal strength through a feeling of direction is a profoundly groundbreaking and individual excursion that resounds across different encounters, societies, and foundations. In the embroidery of human life, people frequently track down that their internal supplies of flexibility, assurance, and backbone are significantly stirred when associated with a higher reason. This investigation dives into the complicated exchange among reason and inward strength, drawing on mental, philosophical, and down to earth aspects to enlighten the groundbreaking likely innate in adjusting one's life to a more profound significance.

At its center, the connection among reason and inward strength is unpredictably woven into the texture of human brain research. The field of positive brain science, spearheaded by analysts like Martin Seligman, underlines the significance of importance and reason in encouraging human prosperity. As indicated by sure brain science, people who see their lives as significant and deliberate are bound to encounter more elevated levels of life fulfillment and in general psychological well-being.

The mental component of finding inward strength through design is exemplified in crafted by Viktor Frankl, a specialist and Holocaust survivor. Frankl's encounters in death camps drove him to create logotherapy, an existential treatment focused on the quest for importance. In his original work, "Man's Quest for Importance," Frankl set that people who track down reason, even despite outrageous affliction, are better prepared to get through difficulties and keep up with inward strength.

Frankl's perceptions highlight the mental versatility that emerges when people interface with a feeling of direction past their nearby conditions. The capacity to get importance from life's difficulties turns into a powerful wellspring of internal strength, empowering people to explore misfortune with a feeling of direction that rises above the limits of their outside conditions.

Also, the connection among reason and inward strength stretches out to the domain of inspiration. Reason fills in as a characteristic inspiration that moves people to define and seek after significant objectives. At the point when people adjust their objectives to a more profound feeling of direction, their inspiration becomes supported and strong.

The quest for reason driven objectives turns into a wellspring of motivation, pushing people to defeat impediments and endure even with misfortunes.

Mentally, reason likewise assumes a vital part in molding character. As people interface with a feeling of direction, they frequently experience an increased identity mindfulness and lucidity about what their identity is and a big motivator for they. This reinforced feeling of personality adds to a strong and versatile self-idea, cultivating internal strength despite outside pressures or cultural assumptions.

From a philosophical point of view, the mission for internal strength through reason lines up with existential beliefs. Existentialism, a philosophical development that stresses individual opportunity, decision, and obligation, places that people get significance from their decisions and activities. Existential rationalists like Jean-Paul Sartre and Albert Camus investigate the possibility that valid living includes effectively making one's motivation instead of capitulating to outside determinism.

Sartre's idea of "dishonesty" features the evasion of credible living when people disregard the obligation of making their own motivation. Conversely, reason driven living lines up with existential standards by underscoring individual organization, decision, and the formation of a daily existence saturated with importance. The existential point of view proposes that internal strength arises when people effectively draw in with the most common way of characterizing and seeking after their motivation.

Existential brain research, as expressed by Viktor Frankl, further underscores the quest for importance as a major part of the human experience. Frankl's logotherapy places that the essential human drive is the quest for significance, and people can find reason even in the most difficult conditions. In the pot of death camps, Frankl saw that the people who recognized a more profound object were bound to endure the dehumanizing conditions.

The existential meaning of direction lies in its capacity to give a structure to facing the existential inquiries of life. Participating in fearless examining — effectively investigating questions regarding presence, reason, and the idea of one's excursion — turns into a philosophical activity that cultivates internal strength. By wrestling with the vulnerabilities of existence with boldness and interest, people conform to the existential mission for validness and deliberate living.

Basically, the excursion of finding internal strength through reason includes purposeful and progressing self-investigation. Commonsense procedures incorporate recognizing fundamental beliefs, investigating interests, putting forth significant objectives, and adjusting everyday activities to a feeling of direction. The incorporation of these functional aspects turns into a guide for people trying to inject their lives with significance and strength.

Values investigation fills in as a central stage in the pragmatic quest for reason. People can think about the qualities that hold importance for them — whether it be genuineness, sympathy, equity, or imagination. Making a rundown and focusing on these qualities gives lucidity about the rules that guide direction and activities. This viable activity lays out serious areas of strength for a for adjusting day to day decisions to a feeling of direction, building up internal strength through the steady encapsulation of basic beliefs.

Energy investigation is another reasonable aspect that includes distinguishing exercises that give veritable pleasure and satisfaction. People can make a rundown of exercises they appreciate and consider when they feel generally enthusiastic and locked in. Perceiving normal subjects or examples in these exercises gives experiences into individual interests. Taking part in reason driven exercises that line up with these interests turns into a viable pathway to implanting day to day existence with a feeling of direction.

Defining reason driven objectives is a pragmatic technique that changes desires into noteworthy stages. By characterizing explicit present moment and long haul objectives that line up with values and interests, people make a guide for individual and expert development. Separating bigger objectives into reachable advances lays out a feeling of deliberate force, cultivating internal strength through purposeful activity and progress.

The common sense of direction stretches out to the formation of a day to day existence vision board — a visual portrayal of one's optimal life and objectives. This innovative activity includes gathering pictures, statements, and images that reverberate with individual desires. Making a composition on a physical or computerized board gives an unmistakable and rousing sign of the imagined future. Routinely returning to and refreshing the vision board turns into a pragmatic ceremony that builds up the association between day to day activities and the overall feeling of direction.

The Japanese idea of Ikigai offers a down to earth structure for tracking down reason by investigating the convergence of what one loves, what one is great at, what the world necessities, and what one can be paid for. Making four records and distinguishing covers between them assists people with pinpointing possible areas of direction. This down to earth blend illuminates choices and activities, directing people toward a comprehensive comprehension of how their interesting characteristics can add to the world.

Creating an individual statement of purpose is a down to earth practice in refining one's motivation into a succinct and effective assertion. Pondering qualities, interests, and long haul objectives, people can draft a statement of purpose that embodies their feeling of direction. Consistently returning to and updating this assertion guarantees that it stays an important and rousing aide in the excursion toward inward strength.

Story reflection, a pragmatic activity including journaling about critical life altering situations, gives a reasonable pathway to understanding the manners by which individual encounters add to one's feeling of direction. Recognizing normal subjects and illustrations learned through these reflections upgrades mindfulness and builds up the account string that shapes one's special story of direction.

The reconciliation of care rehearses into day to day existence offers a commonsense way to deal with improving mindfulness and presence. Care includes developing a condition of uplifted mindfulness and deliberateness. Beginning with short practices, like careful breathing or contemplation, and coordinating care into routine exercises encourages a more profound association with values and reason. Care turns into an establishing practice that adds to internal strength through an increased familiarity with the current second.

Chapter 7

Mindfulness and Inner Peace

In the hurrying around of present day life, where the chaos of day to day requests appears to overwhelm the murmurs of our internal identities, the journey for care and inward harmony has become more critical than any time in recent memory. In a world described by steady network, data over-burden, and a tireless quest for progress, the capacity to develop a feeling of quiet and centeredness has arisen as an encouraging sign for some looking for shelter from the tempest of day to day existence.

Care, at its center, is a condition of dynamic, open consideration regarding the current second. It includes noticing one's contemplations and sentiments without judgment, permitting them to go back and forth like waves on the shore. This training, established in old pensive customs, has tracked down recharged significance in the cutting edge time as a useful asset for exploring the intricacies of the psyche and tracking down comfort amidst mayhem.

The excursion towards care frequently starts with a basic yet significant acknowledgment - that the psyche is an endless stream of contemplations, a downpour of stories and feelings that can divert us from the quietness of the current second. Chasing care, people set out on a way of self-disclosure, figuring out how to unwind themselves from the snare of contemplations that weave their cognizance.

Fundamental to the act of care is the development of mindfulness - an uplifted aversion to the sensations, contemplations, and feelings that emerge in every second. This mindfulness fills in as a directing light, enlightening the inward scene of the brain and offering a more clear comprehension of oneself. Through practices, for example, contemplation and careful breathing, people slowly foster the capacity to moor their regard for the present, cultivating a significant association with the wealth of each passing second.

One of the critical principles of care is the acknowledgment of the current second, no matter what its tendency. This acknowledgment doesn't infer renunciation or resignation yet rather a significant affirmation of reality for what it's worth. It includes embracing both the delights and distresses of existence with composure, perceiving that protection from the present just develops our anguish.

Chasing inward harmony, care goes about as an extension between the outer world and the interior domain of cognizance. It welcomes people to move away from the ceaseless commotion of outer boosts and turn their look internal.

Through this internal excursion, individuals find the huge supply of harmony that exists inside, immaculate by the outside choppiness. It turns into a safe-haven, a shelter where one can withdraw and track down comfort in the midst of the tempests of life.

The advantages of care stretch out past the singular level, saturating into the texture of connections and networks. As people become more sensitive to their own considerations and feelings, they foster an elevated sympathy and comprehension of others. Care cultivates a profound feeling of association, separating the boundaries that frequently independent us from each other. In this interconnectedness, a shared perspective arises, advancing congruity and empathy in the more extensive embroidery of human life.

In any case, the way to care isn't without its difficulties. In a culture that lauds hecticness and accomplishment, cutting out time for thought and self-reflection might appear to be an extravagance. Additionally, the actual idea of the brain - its inclination to meander, to be occupied, and to oppose tranquility - can introduce impressive snags on the excursion towards care. However, it is unequivocally through these difficulties that the extraordinary force of care is uncovered.

Care isn't tied in with accomplishing a static condition of euphoria yet rather a continuous course of development. It is an excursion, not an objective. As people take part in ordinary care rehearses, they foster a versatility that empowers them to explore the recurring pattern of existence with effortlessness. The promising and less promising times fail to be overpowering, and on second thought, become open doors for development and self-revelation.

One of the central standards of care is non-critical mindfulness. As people notice their contemplations and feelings without connecting marks of positive or negative, they make a space for self-sympathy to bloom. This delicate self-acknowledgment turns into a foundation of inward harmony, permitting people to embrace their defects and weaknesses with benevolence.

The act of care frequently interweaves with the idea of reflection, an immortal practice that has been a foundation of different otherworldly and philosophical customs from the beginning of time. Contemplation, in its different structures, fills in as a useful asset for preparing the psyche and extending the act of care. Whether through zeroed in consideration on the breath, cherishing benevolence contemplation, or body check works out, reflection turns into a consecrated space where people can cooperative with the profundities of their being.

In the tranquility of contemplation, the psyche steadily settles, and the chat of considerations starts to die down. It is in this quiet that people experience the embodiment of their reality - a significant mindfulness that rises above the limits of oneself.

This greatness isn't a getaway from the real world but instead an extending of presence, an association with the sweeping cognizance that underlies all of presence.

As people dig into the domains of care and contemplation, they frequently find the interconnected idea of brain and body. The old insight of Eastern practices, like yoga and Judo, stresses the combination of actual stances with breath mindfulness as a way to orchestrate the body and psyche. In the dance of development and breath, specialists experience a feeling of exemplified care, establishing themselves right now through the impressions of the body.

Established researchers has likewise turned its look towards the extraordinary impacts of care on the mind and body. Neuroscientific studies have demonstrated the way that ordinary care practices can prompt underlying changes in the mind, especially in regions related with consideration, feeling guideline, and mindfulness. The pliancy of the mind, when remembered to be bound to early formative stages, is currently perceived as a continuous cycle impacted by experience and purposeful mental preparation.

The physiological advantages of care stretch out past the cerebrum, affecting the autonomic sensory system and the body's pressure reaction. Careful practices, like profound breathing and moderate muscle unwinding, actuate the unwinding reaction, neutralizing the physiological impacts of ongoing pressure. The decrease of pressure chemicals, worked on safe capability, and improved in general prosperity are among the substantial results announced by the people who leave on the excursion of care.

Amidst the logical investigation of care, recognizing its foundations in old insight traditions is critical. Care, in its pith, is definitely not an original idea however an immortal insight that has been gone down through ages. From the lessons of the Buddha on care reflection to the thoughtful acts of emotionless thinkers, the strings of care wind through the embroidery of mankind's set of experiences.

The coordination of care into contemporary helpful methodologies has been a huge improvement in the field of emotional well-being. Care Based Pressure Decrease (MBSR), created by Jon Kabat-Zinn, and Care Based Mental Treatment (MBCT) are proof based mediations that have earned boundless respect for their viability in treating an assortment of emotional wellness conditions, including uneasiness, sorrow, and ongoing torment.

In the helpful setting, care fills in as an instrument for people to foster an alternate relationship with their viewpoints and feelings. As opposed to being snared in the story of misery, people figure out how to notice their psychological examples with an empathetic interest. This change in context makes a space for people to answer difficulties with more prominent clearness and versatility.

The gradually expanding influences of care are apparent in individual prosperity as well as in the authoritative and cultural domains. Ground breaking organizations are integrating care programs into their working environment societies, perceiving the positive effect on worker commitment, innovativeness, and by and large execution.

As care pervades the shared mindset, its capability to cultivate a more empathetic and amicable society turns out to be progressively clear.

Regardless of the developing acknowledgment of the advantages of care, misinterpretations legends actually cover this antiquated practice. One normal confusion is that care is inseparable from unwinding or a detached separation from life. Truly, care is a functioning commitment with the current second, a dynamic and lively mindfulness that imbues each part of existence with increased lucidity.

Another legend encompassing care is that it demands a critical time responsibility or a total way of life upgrade. While formal care rehearses, like reflection, can for sure be tedious, the pith of care lies in the joining of mindfulness into day to day existence. Straightforward demonstrations like careful breathing, enjoying a dinner, or strolling with presence can be strong entryways to care, requiring one minute of deliberate consideration.

All the commodification of care has likewise led to the misguided judgment that it is a convenient solution answer for life's difficulties. Care isn't a panacea however an extraordinary cycle that unfurls over the long haul. The excursion of care requires persistence, devotion, and a readiness to embrace the full range of human experience, from the ordinary to the exceptional.

Chasing care, it is fundamental to perceive that the way is exceptional for every person. What works for one individual may not resound with another. The variety of care rehearses - from care moving through exercises like planting or cooking to the pensive tranquility of situated contemplation - mirrors the flexibility of care to different inclinations and ways of life.

Developing care additionally includes an investigation of the interconnectedness between oneself and the more extensive snare of presence. The natural emergency and the difficulties confronting our planet entice us to extend our care past the limits of individual prosperity to incorporate environmental mindfulness. Care, when applied to our relationship with the Earth, turns into a source of inspiration, rousing dependable stewardship and economical living.

The excursion towards care and internal harmony is certainly not a direct movement yet a nonstop development. There will be epiphanies and snapshots of disarray, seasons of peacefulness and seasons of disturbance. The key is to move toward the excursion with an open heart and a delicate interest, embracing the consistently changing scene of the inward world.

As people explore the territory of their brains, they might experience well established examples of molding, instilled convictions, and unsettled feelings. Care welcomes an empathetic investigation into these layers of oneself, stripping back the cover of deception to uncover the true substance underneath.

In this course of self-revelation, people might uncover torpid possibilities, undiscovered imagination, and a repository of strength that can move them forward on the way of self-improvement.

The combination of care into day to day existence requires a pledge to developing a careful disposition - a mentality of receptiveness, interest, and acknowledgment. This mentality reaches out past proper care practices to pervade the connections, challenges, and delights of regular daily existence. It includes carrying care to the manner in which we impart, connect with others, and draw in with our general surroundings.

In the mission for internal harmony, care turns into a compass, directing people towards a more agreeable relationship with themselves and the world. This excursion isn't tied in with getting away from the intricacies of life yet about tracking down a safe-haven inside, a space of calm strength that stays undisturbed in the midst of the outer disturbance. Inward harmony is certainly not a latent state however a functioning commitment with life, grounded right now and filled by the extraordinary force of care.

As people set out on the excursion towards care and internal harmony, they become modelers of their own prosperity. The material of the brain, once jumbled with the flotsam and jetsam of unexamined considerations, turns into a clean canvas whereupon the craft of careful residing is painted. Every breath, each step, and every second turns into a brushstroke, making a magnum opus of presence and mindfulness.

The products of care mature in the individual space as well as in the shared mindset of mankind. As additional people stir to the groundbreaking capability of care, a gradually expanding influence happens, contacting the existences of everyone around them. Networks imbued with care become cauldrons of sympathy, understanding, and shared prosperity.

In the embroidery of human experience, care arises as a string that meshes together the dissimilar components of life into an agreeable entirety. A string rises above social, strict, and philosophical limits, joining humankind in a common investigation of the internal scene. Through the act of care, people rediscover their interconnectedness with all of presence, perceiving that the mission for inward harmony is an excursion that joins every one of us.

7.1 Introduction to mindfulness and its role in building inner strength

In the steadily speeding up speed of contemporary life, where requests and interruptions flourish, the idea of care has arisen as a guide of quietness and self-disclosure. Established in old thoughtful customs, care is a training that welcomes people to develop an uplifted familiarity with the current second. This dynamic, non-critical consideration regarding the present time and place has earned boundless consideration as a useful asset for cultivating inward strength and versatility notwithstanding life's difficulties.

At its quintessence, care includes the deliberate guiding of one's focus toward the unfurling of the current second. In a world described by consistent boosts and a blast of data, the capacity to zero in on the prompt insight without being cleared away by the flows of interruption is an expertise that holds significant ramifications for mental prosperity.

The excursion into care frequently begins with the acknowledgment of the perpetual chat of the brain. The surge of contemplations, feelings, and responses that possess our psychological scene can turn into a violent stream, diverting us from the quiet shores of the present. Care offers a daily existence pontoon - a way to explore this psychological landscape with purposefulness and presence.

One of the focal precepts of care is the development of mindfulness. This is certainly not a uninvolved perception yet a functioning commitment with the sensations, considerations, and feelings that emerge in every second. Through practices like reflection, careful breathing, or body check works out, people figure out how to notice the variances of their inward scene without becoming caught in the accounts that unfurl.

The meaning of care in developing inward fortitude lies in its capacity to encourage a more profound comprehension of oneself. As people foster the ability to notice their considerations and feelings with non-critical mindfulness, they gain knowledge into the examples of their brain. This mindfulness turns into an establishment for building flexibility, as it permits people to explore life's difficulties with a more prominent feeling of lucidity and understanding.

Fundamental to the act of care is the idea of acknowledgment. It's anything but a detached renunciation to the conditions of life yet a functioning affirmation of reality for all intents and purposes. Right now, people defy the full range of human experience - bliss, distress, energy, and fatigue. Through care, they figure out how to embrace this variety with poise, perceiving that protection from the current second just develops languishing.

The job of care in developing inward fortitude is exemplified in its ability to change the relationship with stress. In the cauldron of day to day existence, stress is an unavoidable buddy, yet not the outside conditions decide its effect yet rather the inward reaction. Care furnishes people with instruments to explore pressure by developing a quiet and focused presence in the midst of the tempest.

Logical examination has started to disentangle the physiological and mental components through which care applies its extraordinary impacts. Neuroscientific studies show the way that customary care practices can prompt primary changes in the mind, especially in regions related with consideration, feeling guideline, and mindfulness. The versatility of the mind, when remembered to be bound to early formative stages, is currently perceived as a continuous cycle affected by experience and purposeful mental preparation.

Notwithstanding its effect on the cerebrum, care stretches out its scope to the body's pressure reaction framework. Careful practices, like profound breathing and reflection, actuate the unwinding reaction, checking the physiological impacts of constant pressure. The decrease of pressure chemicals, worked on invulnerable capability, and upgraded generally speaking prosperity are among the substantial results announced by the individuals who coordinate care into their lives.

While the underlying foundations of care can be followed to old scrutinizing customs, its significance in the contemporary setting is highlighted by its fuse into restorative methodologies. Care Based Pressure Decrease (MBSR) and Care Based Mental Treatment (MBCT) are proof based mediations that have earned respect for their viability in treating an assortment of psychological wellness conditions, including nervousness, despondency, and ongoing torment.

In the helpful setting, care fills in as an instrument for people to foster an alternate relationship with their viewpoints and feelings. As opposed to being trapped in the story of trouble, people figure out how to notice their psychological examples with an empathetic interest. This change in context makes a space for people to answer difficulties with more noteworthy clearness and strength.

The act of care isn't bound to the singular domain; its advantages reach out into the texture of connections and networks. As people become more sensitive to their own contemplations and feelings, they foster an elevated sympathy and comprehension of others. Care encourages a profound feeling of association, separating the hindrances that frequently independent us from each other. In this interconnectedness, a shared perspective arises, advancing congruity and sympathy in the more extensive embroidery of human life.

Notwithstanding the developing acknowledgment of the advantages of care, misinterpretations fantasies actually cover this old practice. One normal confusion is that care is inseparable from unwinding or a detached withdrawal from life. As a general rule, care is a functioning commitment with the current second, a dynamic and lively mindfulness that imbues each part of existence with uplifted lucidity.

Another legend encompassing care is that it demands a huge time responsibility or a total way of life update. While formal care rehearses, like reflection, can to be sure be tedious, the embodiment of care lies in the combination of mindfulness into regular daily existence. Straightforward demonstrations like careful breathing, enjoying a feast, or strolling with presence can be strong passages to care, requiring one minute of purposeful consideration.

All the commodification of care has likewise led to the misguided judgment that it is a handy solution answer for life's difficulties. Care isn't a panacea yet an extraordinary cycle that unfurls over the long haul. The excursion of care requires persistence, devotion, and a readiness to embrace the full range of human experience, from the ordinary to the unprecedented.

Chasing care, it is fundamental to perceive that the way is extraordinary for every person. What works for one individual may not resound with another. The variety of care rehearses - from care moving through exercises like planting or cooking to the insightful tranquility of situated contemplation - mirrors the versatility of care to different inclinations and ways of life.

Developing care likewise includes an investigation of the interconnectedness between oneself and the more extensive snare of presence. The natural emergency and the difficulties confronting our planet allure us to grow our care past the bounds of individual prosperity to incorporate environmental mindfulness. Care, when applied to our relationship with the Earth, turns into a source of inspiration, rousing capable stewardship and reasonable living.

The excursion towards care and inward strength is definitely not a straight movement yet a ceaseless development. There will be breakthrough moments and snapshots of disarray, seasons of peacefulness and seasons of disturbance. The key is to move toward the excursion with an open heart and a delicate interest, embracing the steadily changing scene of the inward world.

As people explore the landscape of their psyches, they might experience firmly established examples of molding, instilled convictions, and unsettled feelings. Care welcomes a humane investigation into these layers of oneself, stripping back the shroud of deception to uncover the genuine quintessence underneath. In this course of self-revelation, people might uncover torpid possibilities, undiscovered imagination, and a supply of flexibility that can drive them forward on the way of self-improvement.

The combination of care into day to day existence requires a promise to developing a careful demeanor - a mentality of transparency, interest, and acknowledgment. This mentality reaches out past proper care practices to penetrate the communications, challenges, and delights of day to day existence. It includes carrying care to the manner in which we convey, connect with others, and draw in with our general surroundings.

In the journey for internal strength, care turns into a compass, directing people towards a more agreeable relationship with themselves and the world. This excursion isn't tied in with getting away from the intricacies of life however about tracking down a safe-haven inside, a space of calm strength that stays undisturbed in the midst of the outside disturbance. Inward strength is definitely not an unbending covering however an adaptable flexibility, grounded right now and energized by the groundbreaking force of care.

As people leave on the excursion towards care and internal strength, they become engineers of their own prosperity. The material of the psyche, once jumbled with the trash of unexamined contemplations, turns into a clean canvas whereupon the specialty of careful residing is painted. Every breath, each step, and every second turns into a brushstroke, making a magnum opus of presence and mindfulness.

The products of care age in the individual space as well as in the shared awareness of mankind. As additional people stir to the extraordinary capability of care, a far reaching influence happens, contacting the existences of everyone around them. Networks mixed with care become pots of empathy.

7.2 Guided mindfulness exercises and practices

Directed care activities and practices act as significant colleagues on the excursion towards developing a more careful and present approach to everyday life. These activities give organized direction and a structure for people trying to coordinate care into their day to day routines. Established in thoughtful customs and adjusted for current settings, these practices offer a different cluster of methods that take special care of different inclinations and ways of life.

One of the fundamental practices in the domain of directed care is careful relaxing. This straightforward yet strong activity includes pointing out centered the breath - the musical breathes in and breathes out that anchor us to the current second. Directed careful breathing activities frequently teach people to notice the vibe of the breath entering and leaving the body, developing a feeling of presence and centeredness.

Careful breathing fills in as a compact anchor, promptly open in snapshots of stress or interruption. By focusing on the breath, people can make a respite in the constant stream of contemplations and feelings, cultivating a snapshot of quiet in the midst of the confusion. Directed care practices in careful breathing might differ in term, permitting specialists to adjust the training to their timetable and inclinations.

Body check contemplation is one more directed care practice that welcomes people to coordinate their consideration efficiently through various districts of the body. In this training, people carry a non-critical attention to sensations, strains, or areas of straightforwardness in each piece of the body. This directed investigation advances a profound association with the current second and assists with delivering physical and mental strain.

As people participate in body filter reflections, they might find region of the body where stress or distress is put away. Through delicate consideration and breath, these pressures can be delivered, adding to a feeling of unwinding and in general prosperity. Directed body filter contemplations are in many cases accessible in changing lengths, making them versatile to various time limitations.

Careful strolling is a training that brings care into movement. In this directed activity, people take part in strolling with conscious and deliberate thoughtfulness regarding each step. The vibes of the feet lifting, traveling through space, and connecting with the ground become a point of convergence for mindfulness. Careful strolling isn't tied in with arriving at an objective however about enjoying the excursion, bit by bit.

Directed care practices in careful strolling can be rehearsed inside or outside, giving adaptability to people to integrate this training into their everyday schedules. The cadenced and monotonous nature of strolling, when joined with careful mindfulness, changes an apparently commonplace movement into a chance for consideration and association with the current second.

Cherishing graciousness contemplation, otherwise called "Metta" reflection, is a directed care practice based on developing a feeling of adoration and empathy towards oneself as well as other people. In this training, people rehash expressions or assertions that express wishes for prosperity, bliss, and harmony. These desires reach out from the self to friends and family, colleagues, and, surprisingly, those with whom there might be struggle.

Directed cherishing thoughtfulness reflections give an organized system to people to sustain sensations of warmth and generosity. By deliberately coordinating positive expectations, people can move their psychological and close to home scene, cultivating a heart-focused way to deal with life. This training isn't tied in with producing explicit feelings yet rather about developing a kind mentality towards oneself and the world.

Care of contemplations and feelings is a directed practice that includes noticing the recurring pattern of considerations and feelings without getting ensnared in their stories. In this activity, people become observers to their psychological cycles, recognizing contemplations and feelings as they emerge and permitting them to condemn. This training develops a roomy and non-receptive consciousness of the psyche.

Directed care practices in care of considerations and feelings furnish people with the apparatuses to unravel themselves from constant examples of reactivity. By fostering a non-critical consciousness of the brain's substance, people can encourage a more offset and knowing relationship with their viewpoints and feelings. This training energizes a feeling of internal quiet in the midst of the vacillations of the psyche.

Careful eating is a directed care practice that focuses on the experience of eating with full mindfulness. In our current reality where dinners are frequently eaten hurriedly in the midst of interruptions, this training urges people to enjoy each chomp, appreciating the flavors, surfaces, and smells of the food. Directed careful eating practices frequently include dialing back the speed of eating, biting intentionally, and focusing on the impressions of yearning and totality.

By participating in careful eating, people can break the programmed designs related with devouring food and foster a more adjusted relationship with sustenance. This training reaches out past the demonstration of eating to an enthusiasm for the interconnectedness between food, the body, and the climate. Directed careful eating practices offer an organized way to deal with developing a careful relationship with food.

Breath mindfulness reflection is a primary directed care practice that focuses on noticing the normal progression of the breath. In this activity, people concentrate on the breath - the ascent and fall of the chest or the vibe of air going through the nostrils. Directed breath mindfulness contemplations frequently consolidate delicate direction to assist people with keeping up with their concentration and return to the breath when the psyche meanders.

Breath mindfulness reflection fills in as an entryway to care, giving people a basic yet strong place of concentration. As specialists become receptive to the breath, they foster an elevated consciousness of the current second and develop a feeling of internal quiet. Directed breath mindfulness contemplations are reasonable for people of all degrees of involvement and proposition an establishment for further developed care rehearses.

Care of sounds is a directed practice that includes focusing on the hear-able scene. In this activity, people become responsive to the sounds around them, whether they are outside clamors or the unpretentious interior hints of the body. Directed care of sounds urges people to tune in without connection or revultion, embracing the hear-able experience as it unfurls.

Directed care practices in care of sounds are versatile to different conditions, making them open in both tranquil and clamoring settings. This training advances an extending of tangible mindfulness and an attunement to the wealth of the current second. By taking part in care of sounds, people can expand their perceptual skylines and foster a more far reaching familiarity with their environmental elements.

The body check contemplation is a directed care practice that includes deliberately coordinating consideration through various region of the body. In this activity, people carry careful attention to every district, noticing sensations, strains, or areas of straightforwardness. Directed body check reflections advance a significant association with the current second and deal a chance for delivering physical and mental strain.

As people participate in body check reflections, they might find region of the body where stress or uneasiness is put away. Through delicate consideration and breath, these pressures can be delivered, adding to a feeling of unwinding and in general prosperity. Directed body examine contemplations are in many cases accessible in fluctuating lengths, making them versatile to various time requirements.

Care of the breath is a directed practice that focuses on pointing out centered the breath. In this activity, people notice the normal cadence of their breath, whether it is the ascent and fall of the chest or the impression of air going through the nostrils. Directed care of the breath practices frequently consolidate delicate direction to help people in keeping up with their concentration and getting back to the breath when the psyche meanders.

Care of the breath fills in as a fundamental practice that can be effortlessly coordinated into day to day existence. Whether rehearsed for a couple of moments or broadened periods, this directed activity offers a place of security amidst the consistently changing flows of the psyche. By securing regard for the breath, people develop a feeling of presence and centeredness.

Directed care practices assume an essential part in making care open and congenial for people at different phases of their excursion. Whether through careful breathing, body check contemplations, or cherishing thoughtfulness rehearses, these directed activities offer an organized pathway to the groundbreaking advantages of care. As people draw in with these practices, they set out on an excursion of self-revelation, creating internal strength, flexibility, and a more significant association with the extravagance of the current second.

7.3 Stories of people who found inner peace through mindfulness

The groundbreaking force of care is proven in the tales of endless people who have left on an excursion of self-revelation and discovered a sense of reconciliation in the midst of life's difficulties. These accounts reverberate with validness and act as tributes to the significant effect of care on mental prosperity, strength, and generally speaking personal satisfaction.

One such story is that of Sarah, a powerful leader exploring the requests of a quick moving professional workplace. Continually shuffling cutoff times, gatherings, and the persistent quest for progress, Sarah ended up trapped in a pattern of pressure and burnout. It was during an especially overpowering period that she coincidentally found care as a likely remedy to her ceaseless mental jabber.

Sarah started integrating short care practices into her day to day daily schedule, beginning with careful breathing during brief breaks and continuously growing to additional lengthy practices. As she became sensitive to the current second, Sarah saw a change in her relationship with stress. As opposed to being consumed by nervousness about the future or second thoughts about the past, she figured out how to secure herself in the present, discovering a feeling of quiet even amidst tumult.

Through predictable care practice, Sarah oversaw pressure all the more successfully as well as found a freshly discovered clearness in her dynamic cycle. The capacity to step back and notice her considerations without prompt response permitted her to answer difficulties with a created and smart disposition. Over the long haul, Sarah's excursion with care brought her inward harmony as well as changed her way to deal with work and life.

Another rousing story is that of James, a battle veteran wrestling with the undetectable injuries of war. Battling with post-horrible pressure problem (PTSD), James confronted the overwhelming undertaking of reintegrating into regular citizen life. Conventional helpful methodologies gave some alleviation, however it was care that offered James a pathway to recovering a feeling of harmony and solidness.

James started with directed care practices zeroed in on breath mindfulness and body filter contemplations. These practices became secures in snapshots of uplifted nervousness, permitting him to ground himself in the present as opposed to being spooky by the recollections of the past. As James proceeded with his care process, he extended his training to incorporate cherishing generosity contemplation, developing empathy towards himself as well as other people.

Care turned into a necessary piece of James' mending interaction, offering him a shelter from the tireless invasion of nosy considerations and feelings. The non-critical mindfulness developed through care permitted him to move toward his encounters with a tenderness that had escaped him previously. James' story embodies the extraordinary capability of care in tending to the complex and nuanced difficulties of psychological wellness recuperation.

In the domain of constant torment the executives, the tale of Maria fills in as a demonstration of the limit of care to ease languishing. Living with a weakening immune system condition, Maria confronted day to day actual agony that swarmed each part of her life. Customary clinical intercessions gave restricted alleviation, inciting Maria to investigate elective methodologies, including care based rehearses.

Through directed care practices that zeroed in on breath mindfulness and body filter reflections, Maria fostered another relationship with her aggravation. As opposed to opposing or dreading the sensations, she figured out how to move toward them with interest and acknowledgment. Care turned into an instrument for Maria to explore the unpredictable interaction between actual distress and profound prosperity.

As Maria proceeded with her care process, she found the idea of "mind-body mindfulness," perceiving the interconnectedness among mental and actual encounters. This mindfulness permitted her to regulate her reaction to torment, diminishing the optional experiencing related with obstruction and close to home misery. Maria's story shows the way that care can engage people to recover organization over their prosperity, even despite ongoing wellbeing challenges.

The story of Imprint, a guardian for a relative with a persistent disease, reveals insight into the job of care in exploring the intricacies of providing care. Confronted with the profound cost of seeing a friend or family member's misery, Imprint ended up sincerely depleted and nearly burnout. Care turned into a life saver, offering him a safe-haven in the midst of the requests of providing care.

Mark began with brief care works out, taking snapshots of quietness during providing care errands to zero in on his breath or participate in short adoring benevolence contemplations. These practices furnished him with a psychological break, permitting him to develop flexibility and sympathy in the midst of the difficulties.

As Imprint extended his care practice, he found a significant change in his ability to be available for his cherished one without being overpowered by the heaviness of the circumstance.

Care turned into a wellspring of restoration for Imprint, empowering him to approach providing care with a feeling of motivation and an open heart. The practices encouraged inward harmony as well as worked with a more profound association with the individual he was really focusing on. Imprint's story delineates the way that care can be an indispensable help for those exploring the sincerely requesting territory of providing care.

With regards to dependence recuperation, the tale of Lisa features the extraordinary capability of care in breaking liberated from the grasp of substance misuse. Battling with a background marked by compulsion, Lisa left on an excursion of recuperation that coordinated care as a focal part. Care works on, including careful breathing and consciousness of desires, became instruments for Lisa to explore the intricacies of compulsion.

Care permitted Lisa to notice the examples of her desires without surrendering to them. The non-critical mindfulness developed through care turned into a counterforce to the disgrace and coerce that frequently go with enslavement. Lisa's care practice reached out past conventional activities to incorporate careful eating, strolling, and other day to day exercises, making a comprehensive way to deal with recuperation.

Through care, Lisa fostered an uplifted aversion to the hidden feelings and triggers that added to her habit-forming ways of behaving. This mindfulness turned into an establishment for pursuing better decisions and answering difficulties with flexibility. Lisa's process embodies the way that care can be a groundbreaking power in habit recuperation, offering a pathway to mending and enduring change.

These accounts of Sarah, James, Maria, Imprint, and Lisa highlight the different manners by which care has filled in as an impetus for inward harmony and change. Whether confronting the tensions of a powerful vocation, exploring the intricacies of emotional well-being, overseeing persistent torment, providing care for a friend or family member, or recuperating from compulsion, these people tracked down comfort and strength through the act of care.

What binds together these stories is the acknowledgment that care is certainly not a one-size-fits-all arrangement yet a flexible and versatile arrangement of instruments. Directed care works out, going from breath attention to body filter contemplations, offer people the adaptability to pick rehearses that resound with their extraordinary necessities and inclinations. The consistency of training, even in a nutshell minutes, turns into the string winding through these accounts of change.

Past the individual domain, these accounts likewise feature the gradually expanding influences of care on relational connections and the more extensive local area. As people develop inward harmony through care, they frequently become guides of empathy, strength, and understanding. The aggregate effect of care stretches out past individual prosperity, adding to a more humane and interconnected society.

These stories welcome reflection on the comprehensiveness of human encounters and the potential for care to act as a wellspring of solidarity and versatility despite life's vulnerabilities. As people keep on sharing their accounts of change through care, the aggregate story of inward harmony turns into a demonstration of the getting through force of presence, mindfulness, and sympathetic self-revelation.

Developing internal harmony through care is a significant excursion that unfurls in the unpredictable scenes of the psyche and the extravagance of the current second. Care, established in old pondering customs, has arisen as a groundbreaking practice that welcomes people to foster an uplifted consciousness of their viewpoints, feelings, and encounters. In the mission for inward harmony, care turns into a directing light, offering a way to explore the intricacies of existence with effortlessness and flexibility.

At the core of care is the craft of presence — the capacity to completely draw in with the current second without being caught in the trap of the past or the projections representing things to come. This deliberate and non-critical mindfulness fills in as an establishment for developing internal harmony by permitting people to observe the unfurling of their lives with lucidity and acknowledgment.

The excursion towards internal harmony through care frequently starts with the breath — a consistently present anchor that grounds people in the promptness of their reality. Breath mindfulness, a key care practice, includes focusing on the normal beat of the breath. In the back and forth movement of inward breaths and exhalations, people find a safe-haven, where the psyche can settle and the choppiness of considerations can die down.

Directed care practices in breath mindfulness give people an organized way to deal with fostering this basic practice. Whether through short snapshots of centered breathing or more expanded contemplation meetings, people figure out how to involve the breath as an extension between the outside world and the inside scene of the brain. The effortlessness of breath mindfulness misrepresents its significant effect on laying out a feeling of quiet and centeredness.

Care goes past the proper act of reflection; it stretches out into the embroidery of regular daily existence. Straightforward demonstrations, when performed with careful consideration, become passages to inward harmony.

Careful eating, for instance, changes the everyday demonstration of devouring food into a tactile encounter. By relishing each chomp, noticing surfaces and flavors, people develop their association with the sustenance that supports them.

Careful strolling, one more epitome of care in day to day existence, welcomes people to step with goal and mindfulness. Every footfall turns into a sign of the current second, a chance to break liberated from the autopilot mode that frequently describes our rushed lives. In the delicate speed of careful strolling, people find that the actual excursion is essentially as critical as the objective.

The idea of inward harmony through care isn't about the shortfall of difficulties or the annihilation of life's challenges. All things considered, it is tied in with fostering a tough and offset relationship with the back and forth movement of life. Care outfits people with the devices to explore pressure, vulnerability, and misfortune with a quiet and consistent presence.

Care of considerations and feelings is a critical part of this excursion. Through directed care works out, people figure out how to notice the changes of their psychological and close to home scene without being cleared away by the flows. This non-receptive mindfulness considers a more profound comprehension of routine examples, molding, and the stories that shape one's emotional experience.

During the time spent care, people frequently experience the layers of oneself — well established convictions, instilled molding, and unsettled feelings. Care welcomes a merciful investigation of these layers, stripping back the shroud of deception to uncover the legitimate embodiment underneath. This excursion of self-disclosure turns into a journey towards internal harmony, as people figure out how to embrace the entirety of their being with generosity and acknowledgment.

Care rehearses, for example, body filter contemplations, work with a significant association with the actual body. In these directed activities, people efficiently guide their focus toward various locales of the body, noticing sensations, pressures, or areas of straightforwardness. The body, frequently a dismissed part of involvement, turns into a point of convergence for developing present-second mindfulness.

The incorporation of care into day to day existence requires a promise to developing a careful disposition — a mentality of transparency, interest, and acknowledgment. This mentality reaches out past proper care practices to penetrate communications, challenges, and delights. Care turns into an approach to connecting with the world — with a responsive heart and a reasonable brain.

The extraordinary capability of care isn't bound to individual prosperity; it reaches out into the texture of connections and networks. As people develop inward harmony through care, they frequently become specialists of empathy, understanding, and shared prosperity. Care turns into a wellspring of association, separating the boundaries that different us from each other.

Logical exploration has started to unwind the physiological and mental systems through which care applies its extraordinary impacts. Neuroscientific studies show the way that ordinary care practices can prompt primary changes in the mind, especially in regions related with consideration, feeling guideline, and mindfulness.

The pliancy of the cerebrum, when remembered to be bound to early formative stages, is currently perceived as a continuous interaction impacted by experience and purposeful mental preparation. Care rehearses, even in short and casual minutes, add to the chiseling of brain processes that help more prominent profound strength, mental adaptability, and generally speaking mental prosperity.

In the restorative domain, care based mediations have earned respect for their viability in treating different psychological wellness conditions. Care Based Pressure Decrease (MBSR) and Care Based Mental Treatment (MBCT) are proof based approaches that incorporate care into remedial settings. These projects have shown progress in decreasing side effects of nervousness, misery, and constant agony.

Care, when applied to the setting of fixation recuperation, turns into a strong partner in breaking liberated from the patterns of hankering and routine ways of behaving. Careful attention to desires permits people to notice the inclinations without prompt reactivity. This non-critical position makes a space for people to answer desires with more noteworthy wisdom and decision.

The development of inward harmony through care in habit recuperation reaches out past the end of substance use; it includes tending to the basic examples of thought and conduct that add to habit-forming cycles. Care turns into a device for people to investigate the main drivers of their misery, cultivating self-empathy and versatility during the time spent mending.

Notwithstanding constant torment, care fills in as a guide of help and self-strengthening. Care based ways to deal with torment the executives stress a change in the relationship with torment, moving from obstruction and repugnance for acknowledgment and understanding. Careful consciousness of torment permits people to explore the sensations with a delicate interest, diminishing the close to home enduring frequently connected with constant agony.

The brain body association, investigated through care, turns into a urgent part of overseeing persistent medical issue. By developing consciousness of the exchange between actual sensations and mental states, people foster a more nuanced comprehension of their prosperity.

Care works on, going from body check reflections to careful development, offer people a collection of instruments for improving their general personal satisfaction.

Care turns out to be especially impactful in the domain of psychological wellness, where the commonness of stress, nervousness, and sadness highlights the requirement for successful survival techniques. The account of people discovering a sense of reconciliation through care with regards to emotional wellness is both motivating and educational.

For people wrestling with nervousness, care fills in as a safe-haven in the midst of the choppiness of dashing considerations and physiological excitement. Care of the breath, specifically, turns into a confided in anchor — a place of center that permits people to ride the floods of uneasiness with more prominent relentlessness. The development of present-second mindfulness offers a respite from the expectant feelings of trepidation that frequently portray uneasiness.

Melancholy, set apart by a feeling of torpidity and profound greatness, finds a contrast in care rehearses that stress delicate development and breath mindfulness. Careful attention to contemplations and feelings furnishes people with devices to investigate the examples of rumination and self-analysis that add to the diligence of burdensome states.

Chapter 8

Building Supportive Relationships

Building steady connections is a diverse and complex cycle that entwines different components of human cooperation. At its center, it includes the development of associations portrayed by sympathy, trust, and shared understanding. These connections assume a critical part in forming the texture of our own and proficient lives, impacting our prosperity, achievement, and generally bliss.

One of the principal mainstays of a strong relationship is successful correspondence. This goes past the simple trade of words; it digs into the specialty of undivided attention, figuring out non-verbal prompts, and articulating one's thoughts with clearness. In the underpinning of each and every solid relationship lies the capacity to impart straightforwardly and truly. At the point when people feel appreciated and comprehended, a feeling of approval penetrates the association, cultivating a climate where trust can thrive.

Trust is the bedrock whereupon strong connections are assembled. A sensitive component finds opportunity to create and can be handily broken. Trust includes not just having faith in the dependability and uprightness of the other individual yet additionally being reliable oneself. Consistency, straightforwardness, and constancy are significant parts in laying out and keeping up with trust. Whenever trust is laid out, people have a good sense of safety in offering their viewpoints and feelings, making a space where weakness is embraced as opposed to dreaded.

Weakness, frequently misinterpreted as an indication of shortcoming, is, truth be told, a strong impetus for building profound associations. At the point when people permit themselves to be defenseless, they make the way for legitimate and significant collaborations. Sharing one's feelings of trepidation, instabilities, and yearnings encourages a feeling of closeness that rises above superficial associations. Through weakness individuals can associate on a significant level, understanding that they are in good company in their battles and wins.

Steady connections are not insusceptible to struggle. Conflicts are a characteristic piece of any human cooperation, and how they are explored can decide the versatility and life span of the relationship. Compromise abilities, in this manner, assume a vital part in keeping a steady unique. The capacity to address contrasts with deference, compassion, and a guarantee to figuring out some shared interest guarantees that clashes become open doors for development instead of wellsprings of division.

Sympathy is the scaffold that associates people on a close to home level. It includes the ability to comprehend and talk about the thoughts of another. In steady connections, sympathy is a foundation, permitting people to associate on a more profound level by perceiving and approving each other's feelings. Compassion cultivates a feeling of kinship and fortitude, causing people to feel seen and grasped, even amidst difficulties.

Developing compassion requires dynamic exertion and a certifiable interest in figuring out the viewpoints of others. It includes venturing into another person's perspective, suspending judgment, and tuning in with an open heart. By embracing sympathy, people can make a climate of empathy that rises above contrasts and encourages a feeling of solidarity.

Notwithstanding compassion, a significant part of building strong connections is the capacity to understand people at their core. This incorporates the capacity to perceive, comprehend, and deal with one's own feelings while likewise being sensitive to the feelings of others. The ability to appreciate people on a profound level empowers people to explore the intricacies of relational elements with responsiveness and mindfulness, laying the preparation for solid and strong associations.

Shared regard is one more key fixing in the recipe for strong connections. It includes esteeming the suppositions, limits, and independence of others. Regard shapes the reason for sound associations, guaranteeing that people feel recognized and appreciated. At the point when regard is available, clashes are drawn closer with a cooperative outlook, and contrasts are praised as opposed to denounced.

Constructing and keeping up with steady connections require a continuous speculation of time and exertion. Like any advantageous undertaking, the profits are corresponding to the responsibility made. This speculation includes being available at the time, effectively captivating with others, and focusing on the relationship in the midst of the requests of day to day existence. Consistency in correspondence and association is fundamental for sustaining a strong security after some time.

While individual endeavors are urgent, the more extensive setting in which connections exist likewise assumes a huge part. Making a steady culture inside families, networks, and associations upgrades the probability of individual connections flourishing. At the point when the climate energizes compassion, open correspondence, and common regard, it gives a rich ground to the development of steady associations.

The job of limits in strong connections couldn't possibly be more significant. Sound limits act as a structure for deferential and equal collaborations. People in strong connections get it and honor each other's limits, perceiving that these limits are fundamental for keeping a healthy identity and independence. Laying out and conveying clear limits encourages a climate where people have a solid sense of reassurance and regarded.

Strong connections stretch out past the individual domain into the expert circle. In the working environment, the elements of strong connections contribute fundamentally to representative prosperity, work fulfillment, and generally efficiency. Pioneers who focus on building steady associations inside their groups establish a good and co-operative workplace, where people feel esteemed and inspired to contribute their best.

Group elements, specifically, benefit tremendously from strong connections among colleagues. Cooperation thrives when there is trust, successful correspondence, and a common obligation to shared objectives. Steady group connections improve imagination and development as well as add to the general achievement and strength of the group notwithstanding difficulties.

Mentorship is a strong sign of steady connections in proficient settings. Coaches give direction, share encounters, and proposition important experiences to those exploring their professions. The coach mentee relationship is based on trust, regard, and a certifiable interest in the development and improvement of the mentee. Through mentorship, people can get to an abundance of information and backing, speeding up their expert process.

Strong connections are likewise necessary to the domain of training. In a learning climate, the association among understudies and educators establishes the vibe for scholastic achievement and self-improvement. Instructors who develop steady associations with their understudies make a positive and enhancing climate where learning goes past the procurement of information to include self-improvement and strengthening.

The effect of steady connections on psychological wellness couldn't possibly be more significant. The feeling of association and having a place that comes from steady connections fills in as a defensive component against stress, uneasiness, and sadness. In the midst of difficulty, having an emotionally supportive network can have a tremendous effect in a singular's capacity to adapt and explore difficulties.

In helpful settings, the restorative union among clients and specialists epitomizes the substance of steady connections. The groundwork of trust and open correspondence is foremost in working with the restorative cycle. Specialists, through their compassionate presence and understanding, make a place of refuge for clients to investigate their feelings and work towards good change.

Social skill is a fundamental part of building steady connections, particularly in the present interconnected and various world. Perceiving and regarding social contrasts upgrades the capacity to associate across different foundations. Socially skillful people explore discussions with awareness, staying away from presumptions and generalizations that can obstruct the advancement of steady connections.

The job of innovation in forming and impacting connections can't be disregarded. While innovation has extended the roads for association, it additionally presents difficulties to the profundity and genuineness of connections. Finding some kind of harmony between advanced correspondence and up close and personal cooperations is urgent to building and supporting steady connections in the cutting edge age.

As friendly creatures, people have a natural requirement for association and having a place. Steady connections satisfy this need, giving a feeling that all is well with the world and importance to people. Dejection and social confinement, then again, can adversely affect mental and actual wellbeing. Perceiving the significance of strong connections, both for individual prosperity and cultural attachment, highlights the requirement for purposeful endeavors in building and sustaining these associations.

Parent-youngster connections address a huge space inside the range of steady associations. The connection among guardians and youngsters lays the foundation for a kid's close to home and mental turn of events. Parental help, portrayed by adoration, direction, and support, cultivates a solid connection that turns into the establishment for sound connections over the course of life.

The meaning of steady connections turns out to be especially obvious during seasons of emergency. Whether confronting individual difficulties, cultural disturbances, or worldwide emergencies, the help of others turns into a life saver. Networks that rally together despite affliction show the versatility and strength that exude from steady associations.

8.1 The importance of relationships in nurturing inner strength

The significance of connections in sustaining inward strength couldn't possibly be more significant. In the perplexing embroidery of human life, the associations we produce with others assume a vital part in forming our close to home strength, confidence, and generally prosperity. These connections, going from familial and kinships to expert and heartfelt, add to the improvement of inward strength - a repository of mettle that enables people to explore life's difficulties with elegance and versatility.

At the core of this idea lies the acknowledgment that people are innately friendly creatures. From the snapshot of birth, people pine for association and look for bonds with others. The early connections shaped inside the nuclear family, especially with guardians or essential parental figures, establish the groundwork for the improvement of the capacity to understand people on a profound level and survival techniques. The sustaining and steady climate given by these underlying connections contribute fundamentally to a singular's feeling that everything is good and self-esteem.

Family connections, specifically, apply a significant effect on the development of internal strength. The nature of the parent-kid relationship, portrayed by affection, care, and reliable help, shapes the youngster's personal establishment. Kids who experience secure connections in their early stages are bound to foster a positive mental self portrait and strength even with life's difficulties. On the other hand, an absence of strong connections inside the family can leave people powerless against profound battles and troubles in adapting to difficulty.

Kinships, frequently viewed as the family we pick, contribute fundamentally to the supporting of internal strength. Real companionships give a feeling of having a place, acknowledgment, and common help. In the midst of happiness, companions gather together to celebrate, and in the midst of distress, they offer comfort and understanding. The fellowship and shared encounters inside kinships make a space where people can be legitimate and helpless, encouraging a feeling of internal strength got from the information that they are in good company in their excursion.

The effect of close connections on internal strength is similarly significant. Cozy organizations include a one of a kind mix of close to home, physical, and mental elements. Solid close connections give a protected base from which people can investigate and explore the difficulties of life. Common help, viable correspondence, and a common obligation to development add to the improvement of strength inside the setting of heartfelt associations.

Proficient connections likewise assume a vital part in forming inward strength. The work environment is a huge field where people experience different characters, explore difficulties, and take a stab at individual and expert development. Steady partners, guides, and bosses add to a positive workplace that improves a singular's feeling of capability and self-esteem. Alternately, harmful or unsupportive work environment connections can disintegrate internal strength, prompting pressure, burnout, and reduced prosperity.

The idea of internal strength is firmly interlaced with close to home versatility - the capacity to return from affliction and adjust to life's difficulties. Steady connections go about as a support against the effect of stressors, giving profound framework that assists people with enduring troublesome times. The consistent encouragement got from connections cultivates a conviction that all is good and soundness, empowering people to confront difficulties with a more prominent feeling of self-control and confidence.

Correspondence inside connections is a foundation of sustaining internal strength. The capacity to offer viewpoints, sentiments, and concerns transparently and truly encourages an environment of trust and understanding. Successful correspondence includes articulating one's own requirements as well as effectively paying attention to the necessities of others. At the point when people feel appreciated and approved inside their connections, it adds to a feeling of strengthening and reinforces the close to home bonds that support inward strength.

Trust, one more essential component of steady connections, is indispensable to the development of internal strength. Trust includes the conviction that others can be depended upon for help, understanding, and consolation. At the point when people trust their connections, they have a real sense of safety in acting naturally, communicating weakness, and looking for direction. This trust turns into a mainstay of solidarity, giving a steady groundwork to self-improvement and strength.

Sympathy, the ability to comprehend and discuss the thoughts of others, is a strong power in cultivating inward strength. At the point when people experience sympathy inside their connections, it makes a feeling of association and approval. Sympathetic connections offer a place of refuge where people can communicate their feelings unafraid of judgment. This close to home approval adds to a powerful identity worth and inward strength.

Developing internal strength through connections includes embracing weakness. The readiness to be open and genuine inside connections permits people to interface on a more profound level. It includes recognizing one's feelings of dread, uncertainties, and flaws without the apprehension about dismissal. Here of weakness, people find that genuine strength lies not in immunity but rather in that frame of mind to be real and authentic.

Compromise abilities inside connections are vital for the upkeep of inward strength. Conflicts and clashes are unavoidable in any human connection. The capacity to explore these contentions with deference, compassion, and a cooperative mentality fortifies the texture of connections. Whenever clashes are drawn nearer as any open doors for development and understanding, instead of as dangers, they add to the improvement of flexibility and internal strength.

Limits inside connections act as a defensive instrument for sustaining internal strength. Sound limits include a reasonable outline of one's necessities, values, and cutoff points. People with clear cut limits are better prepared to keep a healthy identity and safeguard their profound prosperity. Regard for individual limits inside connections establishes a climate where people have a good sense of safety and upheld, encouraging the development of inward strength.

The equal idea of steady connections is apparent in the common advantages determined by all gatherings included. While getting support sustains inward strength, offering help to others additionally adds to self-improvement and flexibility. Thoughtful gestures, sympathy, and backing inside connections make a positive criticism circle, building up the bonds that support internal strength.

With regards to emotional well-being, steady connections assume a crucial part in forestalling and moderating mental trouble. Dejection and social disengagement are risk factors for different emotional well-being conditions, including discouragement and nervousness.

The friendship and consistent encouragement given by connections go about as defensive variables, advancing mental prosperity and adding to the improvement of internal strength.

Helpful connections, framed among people and emotional well-being experts, epitomize the extraordinary force of strong associations. In treatment, the helpful collusion fills in as an impetus for mending and self-awareness. The specialist's compassionate presence, undivided attention, and non-critical help make a space where people can investigate their feelings, gain bits of knowledge, and foster survival techniques, encouraging the development of internal strength.

The significance of connections in supporting internal strength is especially obvious during life changes and significant life altering situations. Whether confronting the difficulties of youth, exploring the intricacies of adulthood, or adapting to misfortune and sorrow, the help of significant connections gives an essential anchor. The common encounters, insight, and close to home food presented by connections guide people through the recurring patterns of life, building up their internal strength.

Social capability inside connections recognizes and regards the variety of encounters and points of view. Perceiving social contrasts improves the capacity to fabricate associations across different foundations. Socially able connections include a receptiveness to finding out about and valuing the uniqueness of every person, adding to a rich embroidery of different associations that encourage internal strength.

The job of connections in sustaining inward strength stretches out to the more extensive cultural setting. Networks that focus on friendly connectedness and backing make an establishment for aggregate flexibility. In the midst of difficulty, for example, cataclysmic events or cultural difficulties, the strength of networks lies in the bonds produced through connections. The common guide, collaboration, and fortitude inside networks epitomize the groundbreaking force of strong associations.

All in all, the significance of connections in supporting internal strength is a demonstration of the significant effect of human associations on the texture of our lives. From the support to advanced age, connections shape our personality, give a feeling of having a place, and add to the strength that permits us to explore the intricacies of the human experience. Through correspondence, trust, sympathy, and a guarantee to shared development, people can develop and support inward strength inside the embroidery of interconnected connections that characterize the quintessence of being human.

8.2 Strategies for fostering healthy and supportive connections

Encouraging sound and strong associations is a dynamic and purposeful interaction that contributes essentially to generally prosperity. These associations, whether individual or expert, structure the foundation of a satisfying and significant life.

Constructing and keeping up with such connections require a blend of mindfulness, powerful correspondence, and a promise to common development. In this investigation of procedures for encouraging solid and strong associations, we dig into different viewpoints that add to the development of hearty and positive connections.

Vital to the undertaking of encouraging sound associations is the development of mindfulness. Figuring out one's own qualities, requirements, and limits lays the preparation for valid and satisfying connections. Mindfulness includes pondering individual qualities, regions for development, and the examples of conduct that shape collaborations with others. By acquiring understanding into their own feelings, people can explore associations with a more noteworthy feeling of clearness and reason.

Powerful correspondence fills in as the foundation of solid associations. It includes offering one's viewpoints and sentiments as well as effectively paying attention to other people. Correspondence is a two-way road, requiring both talking and tuning in with deliberateness. The specialty of undivided attention includes being completely present, suspending judgment, and trying to figure out the viewpoints of others. At the point when people feel appreciated and comprehended, the establishment for a solid and strong association is laid out.

Defining and regarding limits is pivotal for cultivating solid associations. Limits characterize the boundaries of satisfactory way of behaving and assist with keeping a feeling of individual independence inside connections. Clear and imparted limits make a place of refuge where people feel regarded and comprehended. Regarding the limits of others is similarly significant, as it lays out a groundwork of trust inside the relationship.

Building trust is a progressive interaction that requires consistency, straightforwardness, and dependability. Trust shapes the bedrock of solid associations, affecting the degree of weakness people will communicate. Trust is worked through the arrangement of words and activities, the show of dependability, and the affirmation of shared values. Once settled, trust adds to a feeling of safety and transparency inside the relationship.

Developing compassion is fundamental for cultivating solid associations. Compassion includes the capacity to comprehend and discuss the thoughts of others. It requires venturing into another person's point of view, perceiving their feelings, and answering with sympathy. Compassionate associations make a space for shared understanding and approval, cultivating a feeling of association and backing.

With regards to encouraging sound associations, inspiration and appreciation assume an extraordinary part. Energy includes developing a hopeful mentality and zeroing in on the qualities and positive parts of the relationship. Offering thanks for the presence and commitments of others improves the general inspiration inside the association. Appreciation fills in as an integral asset for supporting the worth and meaning of the relationship.

Powerful compromise is an expertise that adds to the life span and strength of associations. Clashes are unavoidable in any relationship, and how they are tended to can either fortify or strain the association. Solid compromise includes moving toward conflicts with deference, undivided attention, and a guarantee to figuring out some mutual interest. Seeing struggles as any open doors for development instead of as dangers to the relationship encourages strength and understanding.

Putting time and exertion into the relationship is a major technique for cultivating solid associations. Connections require sustaining and consideration regarding flourish. Ordinary correspondence, quality time spent together, and shared encounters add to the imperativeness of the association. Focusing on the relationship in the midst of the requests of day to day existence exhibits a promise to its development and manageability.

In the computerized age, where innovation assumes a huge part in correspondence, finding some kind of harmony among virtual and eye to eye interactions is fundamental. While innovation gives advantageous ways of associating, the extravagance of in-person correspondence ought to be acknowledged with a sober mind. Eye to eye collaborations consider non-verbal signs, profound subtleties, and a more profound degree of association that computerized correspondence might need.

Social capability is crucial for cultivating solid associations in a different and inter-connected world. Perceiving and regarding social contrasts improves the capacity to construct significant associations across different foundations. Social ability includes a receptiveness to finding out about and valuing the uniqueness of every person, cultivating a comprehensive and steady climate.

The act of dynamic appreciation adds to the encouraging feedback of sound associations. Communicating appreciation for the characteristics, activities, and commitments of others reinforces the security inside the relationship. Routinely recognizing and saying thanks to people for their presence and backing makes a positive and confirming environment.

Establishing a steady climate inside the relationship includes being receptive to the necessities and goals of the other individual. Supporting their objectives, offering consolation, and commending their accomplishments add to a feeling of common strengthening. Thus, feeling upheld upgrades the singular's certainty and flexibility inside the association.

With regards to familial connections, ceremonies and customs assume a huge part in cultivating association and a feeling of having a place. Shared ceremonies, whether they include festivities, family feasts, or other significant exercises, make a feeling of coherence and shared history. These ceremonies act as anchors, establishing the family in a common character and building up the bonds that interface its individuals.

Careful correspondence is a procedure that advances purposefulness and presence inside associations. Care includes being completely present at the time, liberated from interruptions and predispositions. Applying care to correspondence upgrades the nature of collaborations, extends understanding, and cultivates a feeling of associa-tion. Careful correspondence includes monitoring one's words, tone, and non-verbal prompts, adding to a more legitimate and strong association.

The act of pardoning is an indispensable part of encouraging solid associations. Connections definitely experience difficulties and clashes, and holding onto disdain can disintegrate the texture of the association. Absolution includes relinquishing feel-ings of resentment, developing compassion, and looking for understanding. A ground-breaking demonstration adds to the mending and flexibility of the relationship.

Keeping a solid balance between fun and serious activities is essential for cultivat-ing positive associations, especially in proficient settings. The requests of the work environment can now and again encroach on private time and connections. Laying out limits among work and individual life, focusing on taking care of oneself, and cultivating a steady workplace add to the general prosperity and supportability of associations.

In proficient connections, mentorship fills in as a significant technique for en-couraging development and improvement. Tutors give direction, share encounters, and proposition important experiences to those exploring their professions. Mentor-ship connections are described by common regard, trust, and a common obligation to learning and development. The tutor mentee dynamic adds to the expert turn of events and strength of people inside the association.

Social encouraging groups of people are instrumental in cultivating solid associations and giving a feeling of local area. Fabricating and keeping up with associations inside a more extensive informal organization offer different viewpoints, shared assets, and a feeling of having a place. Social encouraging groups of people act as security nets during testing times and add to the general flexibility and prosperity of people.

Solid associations stretch out past individual connections to the more extensive local area and cultural levels. Local area commitment and inclusion add to a feeling of association and reason. Partaking in local area exercises, chipping in, and adding to shared objectives cultivate a feeling of having a place and reinforce the social texture of the local area.

Schooling and mindfulness working about solid relationship elements are fundamental techniques for encouraging steady associations. Furnishing people with the information and abilities to develop solid connections adds to a culture of shared regard and understanding. Instructive drives on viable correspondence, compromise, and the ability to understand people on a profound level engage people to explore associations with deliberateness and sympathy.

The job of administration is urgent in cultivating solid associations inside associations. Pioneers set the vibe for the hierarchical culture, affecting the nature of expert connections. Pioneers who focus on correspondence, straightforwardness, and the prosperity of their colleagues add to a positive and steady workplace. Thusly, representatives feel esteemed, persuaded, and associated with the more extensive objectives of the association.

Advancing a culture of inclusivity and variety inside connections is an essential goal. Comprehensive conditions embrace and celebrate contrasts, encouraging a feeling of having a place for people from different foundations. Procedures, for example, racial awareness coaching, comprehensive approaches, and setting out open doors for different voices to be heard add to the making of strong associations that rise above.

8.3 Personal stories illustrating the impact of positive relationships on inner strength

Individual stories clearly represent the extraordinary force of positive connections in molding and bracing inward strength. These stories, drawn from assorted encounters, feature the significant effect that steady associations can have on a singular's versatility, confidence, and by and large prosperity. Through these accounts, we gain experiences into the manners by which positive connections act as mainstays of solidarity, giving comfort, consolation, and a feeling of having a place.

One impactful story unfurls in the domain of familial connections, where the connection between a parent and kid turns into a wellspring of enduring help. Sarah, a young lady exploring the difficulties of youthfulness, wound up wrestling with weaknesses and self-question. It was her mom, Emily, who arose as a directing light during this wild period. Emily, perceiving the significance of encouraging her girl's internal strength, participated in transparent correspondence.

Through sincere discussions, Emily made a place of refuge for Sarah to communicate her feelings of trepidation and vulnerabilities. Emily's compassionate tuning in and enduring help turned into a consistent starting point for Sarah's confidence. As Sarah explored the intricacies of youthfulness, her mom's consolation filled in as a wellspring of motivation, supporting her faith in her own capacities. The positive connection among Sarah and her mom turned into an imperative impetus for the improvement of Sarah's inward strength, engaging her to confront life's difficulties with flexibility and an identity worth.

In the domain of companionships, the narrative of David and Michael shows the extraordinary effect of common help. David, a youthful expert exploring the requests of a difficult vocation, tracked down comfort and strength in his companionship with Michael. The two companions, notwithstanding the geological distance that isolated them, kept a reliable and steady association through normal assembles and virtual conferences.

During an especially requesting gradually ease in David's profession, Michael's consolation and understanding turned into a life saver. Michael, himself acquainted with the tensions of the expert world, gave a listening ear, key guidance, and unfaltering support. The positive and steady nature of their fellowship permitted David to explore business related burdens with a feeling of point of view and versatility. The brotherhood among David and Michael braced David's inward strength as well as exemplified the extraordinary force of strong fellowships even with proficient difficulties.

In the domain of close connections, the tale of Maria and Alex highlights the effect of a solid organization on individual prosperity. Maria, a youthful expert with aggressive vocation objectives, ended up in a heartfelt connection with Alex, a steady and compassionate accomplice. As Maria experienced profession related difficulties and snapshots of self-question, Alex's unflinching help and faith in her capacities turned into a foundation of her inward strength.

In the midst of expert difficulties, Alex's consolation and pragmatic help reinforced Maria's flexibility. The positive elements inside their relationship made a space where weakness was embraced, and challenges were seen as any open doors for development. Maria's excursion, set apart by the help of a cherishing and certifying accomplice, embodies how positive heartfelt connections can act as anchors of solidarity, adding to a singular's general prosperity and confidence.

The expert circle gives a background to one more convincing story, where the mentorship connection among Sarah and James turns into an impetus for individual and profession development. Sarah, a youthful expert exploring the complexities of a serious industry, wound up under the mentorship of James, an accomplished and old pro. James, perceiving the potential inside Sarah, became a guide as well as a steady backer for her expert turn of events.

Under James' direction, Sarah encountered a groundbreaking excursion of learning, expertise improvement, and professional success. James' support, helpful criticism, and confidence in Sarah's capacities became essential variables in the development of her internal strength. The mentorship relationship, portrayed by trust and backing, moved Sarah's vocation as well as contributed fundamentally to her identity viability and versatility even with proficient difficulties.

With regards to emotional well-being, the account of Imprint highlights the effect of steady connections on one's capacity to explore and beat affliction. Mark, confronting a time of personal unrest and uneasiness, tracked down comfort in the friendship of his dear companion, Lisa. Lisa's sympathetic presence and non-critical help made a place of refuge for Imprint to share his battles and look for understanding.

As Imprint set out on an excursion of treatment to address his emotional wellness challenges, Lisa's steady help filled in as a balancing out force. Her readiness to go with Imprint to treatment meetings, offer consolation, and celebrate little triumphs became instrumental in Imprint's

recuperating cycle. The positive and steady connection among Imprint and Lisa represents the essential job that comprehension and compassionate associations play in cultivating mental prosperity and inward strength.

The account of Jenna and her steady local area outlines the aggregate effect of positive connections on individual versatility. Jenna, a single parent confronting the difficulties of bringing up a kid while seeking after her schooling, ended up embraced by a local area of companions, neighbors, and coaches. This steady organization gave not just pragmatic help, like childcare and scholarly help yet in addition close to home consolation and approval.

Jenna's excursion, set apart by the aggregate help of her local area, embodies the groundbreaking force of positive connections even with complex life conditions. The organization of associations developed by Jenna turned into a wellspring of solidarity, empowering her to explore the crossing point of being a parent and instruction with strength and assurance. The account of Jenna and her local area highlights the public idea of help and its significant effect on individual prosperity.

With regards to social variety, the tale of Ahmed and Mei offers a brief look into the groundbreaking capability of diverse associations. Ahmed, a global understudy, ended up exploring the difficulties of adjusting to another social climate. Mei, a neighborhood understudy with a profound appreciation for social variety, stretched out a hand of kinship to Ahmed.

Through their companionship, Ahmed not just tracked down useful help in exploring the subtleties of another culture yet in addition encountered a feeling of having a place and acknowledgment. Mei's receptiveness to finding out about Ahmed's social foundation and her eagerness to share her own social encounters made a steady and improving association. The positive connection among Ahmed and Mei shows how multifaceted associations can add to a feeling of having a place and internal strength, rising above geological and social limits.

The story of Tom, a tactical veteran, outlines the effect of kinship and shared encounters in cultivating internal strength. Tom, having served in testing and requesting conditions, found comfort and backing in the bonds shaped with his kindred veterans. The common encounters, understanding, and shared help inside the veteran local area turned into a vital part of Tom's excursion toward recuperating and versatility.

The positive connections manufactured during Tom's tactical help offered profound help as well as filled in as a sign of the strength that rises up out of shared difficulty. The fellowship inside the veteran local area embodies how shared encounters and understanding add to the development of inward strength, especially notwithstanding one of a kind difficulties related with military help.

In the story of Emily, an overcomer of abusive behavior at home, the extraordinary effect of steady connections on the way to mending comes to the front. Emily, having gotten away from a harmful relationship, tracked down comfort in the strong organization of companions, family, and experts. The sympathetic grasping, approval, and useful help offered by her help framework became necessary to her excursion toward recuperation.

The positive connections inside Emily's organization offered basic reassurance as well as assumed an essential part in her admittance to assets and administrations. The aggregate strength of her emotionally supportive network turned into an encouraging sign, enabling Emily to reconstruct her life and recover a feeling of organization. The account of Emily shows the significant effect that strong connections can have on people exploring the intricacies of injury and recuperation.

These individual stories aggregately highlight the groundbreaking force of positive connections in supporting and sustaining inward strength. Whether inside familial securities, companionships, close connections, mentorships, networks, or diverse associations, the consistent idea is the significant effect of steady elements on individual prosperity. These stories embody how sympathy, figuring out, support, and shared encounters add to the development of versatility and a vigorous identity.

In every story, positive connections act as impetuses for self-improvement, strengthening, and the defeating of misfortune. The stories feature the job of steady associations in giving a feeling of having a place, approval, and profound food. Whether through the relentless help of a parent, the kinship of companions, the support of a tutor, or the aggregate strength of a local area, these accounts epitomize the groundbreaking.

The significant effect of positive connections on internal strength is a story that unfurls across the range of human encounters. From the close obligations of familial connections to the steady embroidery of companionships and the groundbreaking elements of heartfelt associations, the narratives of people are permeated with the extraordinary force of good connections. Inside these stories, the strings of sympathy, trust, and shared encounters wind around together to sustain inward strength, adding to flexibility, confidence, and in general prosperity.

Consider the narrative of Emma, a young lady exploring the difficulties of immaturity. Amidst self-disclosure and the mission for personality, Emma tracked down comfort and support inside the folds of her familial connections. The unfaltering help of her folks, described by open correspondence, understanding, and a non-critical hug, turned into a wellspring of solidarity during snapshots of self-question. Through the positive elements inside her family, Emma developed a powerful identity worth and versatility, laying the preparation for exploring the intricacies of existence with certainty.

The effect of positive familial connections on inward strength is additionally exemplified by the tale of Daniel, who, in spite of confronting misfortune, drew strength from the steady hug of his kin. Daniel's excursion, set apart by familial bonds described by adoration, common help, and shared values, gave a balancing out force during testing times. The fellowship and understanding inside his family filled in as a mainstay of solidarity, cultivating strength and a feeling of having a place.

The story of Alice and her persevering through companionship with Sarah reveals insight into the extraordinary idea of positive associations outside the domain of family. Sarah, confronting the preliminaries of adulthood and the tensions of a requesting vocation, tracked down comfort and grasping in her fellowship with Alice. The correspondence of their help, set apart by compassionate tuning in, shared chuckling, and common consolation, turned into a foundation of their singular strength. The kinship among Alice and Sarah embodies the meaning of positive connections in giving close to home food and bracing inward strength.

In the domain of close connections, the narrative of Michael and Olivia shows the groundbreaking effect of a sound organization. Olivia, exploring the recurring patterns of life, found in Michael a strong and certifying accomplice. Michael's faithful confidence in Olivia's capacities, combined with a common obligation to development and shared understanding, made a relationship portrayed by trust and strengthening. The positive elements inside their heartfelt association turned into a wellspring of inward strength for both Michael and Olivia, representing the extraordinary force of steady organizations.

Proficient connections, frequently a huge part of grown-up life, add to the development of inward strength. The story of Alex, a youthful expert exploring the intricacies of the working environment, unfurls against the setting of a mentorship relationship with Lauren. Lauren, an accomplished and steady tutor, gave direction, useful criticism, and consolation. The mentorship dynamic turned into an impetus for Alex's expert development, contributing not exclusively to professional success yet in addition to the improvement of versatility and self-viability.

Inside the setting of psychological well-being, the narrative of Hannah shows the effect of positive helpful connections on internal strength. Hannah, confronting the difficulties of uneasiness and discouragement, set out on a remedial excursion with Dr. Patel. The sympathetic and non-critical help given by Dr. Patel made a remedial collusion that turned into a foundation of Hannah's mending interaction. The positive restorative relationship added to side effect help as well as cultivated a feeling of strengthening and versatility despite psychological well-being difficulties.

The story of James, a tactical veteran, reveals insight into the exceptional elements of kinship and shared encounters in forming internal strength. James, having served in testing and requesting conditions, found in the bonds shaped with his kindred veterans a wellspring of understanding and backing.

The common encounters inside the veteran local area turned into a demonstration of the extraordinary force of positive associations in cultivating flexibility and a feeling of mutual perspective.

Multifaceted connections, as exemplified by the narrative of Aisha and Carlos, feature the improving effect of variety on inward strength. Aisha, a worldwide under-study, found in Carlos a companion who embraced and celebrated social contrasts. The positive multifaceted association not just furnished Aisha with a feeling of having a place yet additionally added to her self-awareness and versatility in exploring another social setting.

With regards to recuperation and strength, the account of Imprint outlines the effect of positive associations in beating difficulty. Mark, an overcomer of habit, tracked down strength and backing inside a local area of people on a comparable excursion. The aggregate getting it, sympathy, and shared obligation to recuperation inside the encouraging group of people became indispensable to Stamp's excursion toward versatility and inward strength.

The story of Rachel, a solitary parent exploring the intricacies of bringing up a kid, highlights the common idea of help. Rachel's insight, set apart by the hug of a steady local area, embodies how positive connections inside a more extensive organization add to individual prosperity. The aggregate strength of the local area turned into a wellspring of versatility for Rachel, empowering her to explore the requests of being a parent sincerely and a feeling of shared liability.

These different stories by and large enlighten the manners by which positive connections add to the development of internal strength. Inside the embroidery of human encounters, the strings of trust, sympathy, shared encounters, and common help wind around together to frame a texture that strengthens people despite life's difficulties. Whether inside the private obligations of family, the strong hug of fellow-ships, the groundbreaking elements of heartfelt associations, or the kinship inside expert and remedial connections, good associations act as anchors that support and support inward strength.

Additionally, these stories accentuate the corresponding idea of positive connec-tions. The effect of strong associations stretches out past individual prosperity to add to the strength and versatility of the more extensive local area. With regards to families, companionships, heartfelt organizations, mentorships, and networks, the good elements inside connections make a far reaching influence, cultivating a culture of figuring out, sympathy, and aggregate strength.

The extraordinary force of positive connections is additionally highlighted by their part in molding one's feeling of personality and self-esteem. The stories introduced here show how the confirmation, consolation, and faith in one's capacities inside strong connections add to the improvement of a hearty and positive self-idea.

The effect of positive connections isn't restricted to snapshots of challenge; rather, it turns into a necessary part of a person's continuous excursion toward self-improvement and satisfaction.

The meaning of correspondence inside certain connections arises as an ongoing idea in these stories. Whether communicated through open discussions inside families, the common comprehension between companions, the common goals inside heartfelt associations, or the direction gave in mentorship connections, viable correspondence fills in as a key part in the development of good elements. The capacity to communicate needs, share weaknesses, and listen sympathetically turns into a foundation of the extraordinary effect of positive connections on inward strength.

Trust, one more key component inside sure connections, is woven into the texture of these stories. The trust laid out inside familial bonds, companionships, heartfelt associations, and expert connections turns into an establishment whereupon people can depend in the midst of vulnerability. Trust isn't just a result of positive connections yet additionally a contributing component to the versatility and inward strength developed inside these associations.

Compassion, a common subject in these accounts, stands apart as a strong power in cultivating positive connections. The capacity to comprehend and discuss the thoughts of others makes a feeling of association and approval. The stories represent how compassion inside connections fills in as an impetus for recuperating, self-improvement, and the improvement of internal strength. In snapshots of weakness, the presence of compassionate comprehension turns into a groundbreaking power, adding to a singular's feeling of being seen, heard, and esteemed.

Chapter 9

Sustaining Whispers of Inner Strength

In the tremendous embroidery of human life, there exists a fragile transaction between the outside world and the inner domain of contemplations and feelings. Inside the openings of the human spirit, there are murmurs - unpretentious yet significant reverberations that resound with the pith of internal strength. These supporting murmurs, frequently muffled by the whirlwind of life's difficulties, hold the ability to direct and strengthen the soul even with affliction.

Life, in its horde structures, presents an unpredictable dance of euphoria and distress, win and rout. It is an excursion that we leave upon with the material of our reality clear, yet progressively painted by the strokes of our encounters. In the midst of the wild oceans of progress, the supporting murmurs of internal strength arise as a consistent beacon, enlightening the way through the most obscure evenings of the spirit.

The beginning of inward strength lies in the pot of self-disclosure. As we explore the maze of our own cognizance, we experience parts of ourselves that are tough, fearless, and unfaltering. These aspects, frequently clouded by the shadows of self-uncertainty and outer tensions, anticipate acknowledgment and affirmation. The supporting murmurs allure us to dig into the profundities of our being, to uncover the lethargic repositories of solidarity that lie torpid inside.

However, the excursion of self-revelation isn't without its difficulties. The wild flows of life might clear us away, leaving us unfastened in an ocean of vulnerability. It is at these times of weakness that the supporting murmurs become a help, delicately pushing us towards the shores of versatility. Internal strength is definitely not a static substance; a unique power develops and develops with every preliminary confronted and survive.

In the embroidery of life, connections structure the complex strings that weave the texture of our reality. The supporting murmurs of internal strength find reverberation in the bonds we manufacture with others. A common look, a soothing touch, or a basic expression of support can fuel the blazes of versatility inside. It is in the cauldron of human association that the genuine force of inward strength is uncovered, for it's anything but a single power however an aggregate energy that ties hearts and spirits together.

The supporting murmurs of inward strength reverberation through the passages of time, resounding in the tales of the people who have confronted unconquerable chances and arisen triumphant. History, with its embroidery of wins and hardships, is a demonstration of the dauntless human soul. From the indifferent purpose of people who faced the hardships of misfortune to the aggregate strength of networks that miraculously rose like a phoenix after despair, the supporting murmurs resound across ages, moving expectation and versatility.

In the cutting edge time, where the speed of life is frantic and the requests on people are unremitting, the supporting murmurs of internal strength are in many cases muffled by the commotion of outer assumptions. The quest for progress, the tensions of similarity, and the constant walk of time can cloud the inborn supplies of solidarity that exist in. In the mission for outer approval, the murmurs are quieted, and the soul is left dry and longing.

Society, with its bunch standards and principles, frequently forces a story that characterizes strength in tight terms - an emotionless disposition, steadfast purpose, and an enduring outside. However, the supporting murmurs of internal strength resist such inflexible definitions. Genuine strength lies not in that frame of mind of weakness but rather in the hug of realness. It is in recognizing our feelings of dread, questions, and uncertainties that we tap into the wellspring of versatility inside.

The supporting murmurs of inward strength are a call to credibility, an enticing towards a more profound association with oneself. In a world that commends flaw-lessness and achievement, the boldness to be blemished and powerless turns into an extreme demonstration of disobedience. It is in the acknowledgment of our defects and flaws that we find the genuine substance of solidarity - a strength that is conceived not out of refusal however out of confidence and self-empathy.

The excursion towards supporting internal strength is certainly not a direct way however a wandering investigation of oneself. A journey requests thoughtfulness, self-reflection, and a readiness to face the shadows that hide inside. The supporting murmurs guide us through the maze of our own mind, encouraging us to go up against the devils that repress our development and self-disclosure.

Chasing internal strength, versatility arises as a sturdy friend. Like a durable anchor in the whirlwind of life, versatility grounds us despite difficulty. It isn't the shortfall of moves however the capacity to return from misfortunes that characterizes flexibility. The supporting murmurs advise us that mishaps are not inseparable from disappoint-ment yet are venturing stones towards development and self-acknowledgment.

The supporting murmurs of inward strength are not restricted to snapshots of emergency; they penetrate the texture of regular daily existence. It is in the little triumphs, the snapshots of euphoria, and the calm victories that the murmurs are generally unmistakable.

The capacity to find strength in the customary is a demonstration of the flexibility that dwells inside the human soul. A strength changes the unremarkable into the uncommon and injects the daily schedule with a feeling of direction and importance.

The excursion towards supporting inward strength is indistinguishable from the development of a positive outlook. In the nursery of the psyche, the seeds of energy bloom into the blossoms of strength. The supporting murmurs guide us in watching out for the nursery of our viewpoints, getting rid of cynicism and sustaining the seeds of hopefulness. A positive outlook isn't a forswearing of reality yet a cognizant decision to zero in on the conceivable outcomes and open doors that exist in each test.

Chasing after supporting internal strength, the job of taking care of oneself couldn't possibly be more significant. The supporting murmurs advocate for an all encompassing way to deal with prosperity - a sustaining of the body, psyche, and soul. Taking care of oneself isn't an extravagance however a crucial support point whereupon the structure of internal strength is constructed. It is a guarantee to sustaining oneself, genuinely, inwardly, and profoundly, in order to develop the versatility expected to explore the rhythmic movement of life.

As we navigate the scene of our lives, the supporting murmurs of internal strength entice us to develop an outlook of appreciation. In the embroidery of endowments and difficulties, appreciation arises as a string that ties the texture of our reality. It is in offering thanks for the snapshots of satisfaction, the examples learned, and the versatility acquired that we weave a story of solidarity and determination.

The supporting murmurs of inward strength track down reverberation in the force of care. In a world that frequently pulls us in bunch headings, care turns into a compass that guides us back to the current second. It is in the quietness of care that we hear the murmurs most plainly, for it is right now that the embodiment of internal strength is felt. Care is certainly not a transient practice however an approach to being - a cognizant mindfulness that injects each breath and each step with expectation and reason.

In the embroidered artwork of human experience, the supporting murmurs of internal strength are entwined with the subject of flexibility. Strength is definitely not a quality held for a limited handful yet a limit that dwells inside every person. It is the capacity to adjust, return, and flourish even with misfortune. The supporting murmurs guide us in tackling the force of strength, for it is through versatility that we change difficulties into impetuses for development.

The supporting murmurs of inward strength reverberation through the passages of weakness. It is in recognizing our weaknesses that we tap into the wellspring of solidarity inside. Weakness isn't a shortcoming yet an entryway to realness and association. The supporting murmurs welcome us to embrace our weaknesses, for it is in the hug that we find the flexibility that lies underneath the surface.

In the excellent embroidery of life, the supporting murmurs of inward strength find articulation in the specialty of giving up. Giving up isn't an acquiescence however a delivery - an arrival of connections, assumptions, and the requirement for control. It is in the giving up that we free ourselves from the weights that overload us, permitting the supporting murmurs to direct us towards a lighter, more freed presence.

The supporting murmurs of internal strength entice us to develop a feeling of interest and transparency. Life is an unending excursion of revelation, and it is in the receptiveness to new encounters, viewpoints, and potential outcomes that we tap into the vast repositories of internal strength. The supporting murmurs are a call to wander past the natural, to investigate the unfamiliar regions of our true capacity.

In the midst of the hardships of life, the supporting murmurs of internal strength track down comfort in the force of association. Human association, whether through connections, local area, or shared encounters, is a wellspring of solidarity and versatility. It is in the aggregate embroidery of humankind that the supporting murmurs become an ensemble, resounding with the common battles and wins of people and networks.

The supporting murmurs of internal strength welcome us to hit the dance floor with the vulnerabilities of life. In a world that is steadily changing and eccentric, the capacity to explore the obscure turns into a significant part of versatility. The supporting murmurs guide us in embracing vulnerability not as a danger but rather as a material whereupon the show-stopper of our lives unfurls.

9.1 Recap of key concepts from previous chapters

The excursion we have left upon has taken us through the perplexing embroidered artwork of human experience, investigating the supporting murmurs of internal strength that reverberate inside the profundities of the human spirit. As we explore the exciting bends in the road of life, the embodiment of inward strength uncovers itself in different topics and ideas that have been woven into the texture of our investigation.

At the core of our process lies the idea of self-revelation. The supporting murmurs of internal strength allure us to dig into the openings of our own awareness, asking us to uncover the strong, gutsy, and immovable parts of ourselves. Self-disclosure is certainly not a static cycle yet a continuous investigation that requires thoughtfulness, self-reflection, and an eagerness to stand up to the shadows that might prowl inside. It is through this cycle that we come to perceive and recognize the lethargic repositories of solidarity that lie underneath the surface.

A pivotal part of supporting internal strength is the acknowledgment of weakness as a wellspring of realness and association. The supporting murmurs guide us in embracing our weaknesses, understanding that they are not shortcomings but rather passages to a more profound comprehension of ourselves as well as other people.

It is in the affirmation of our feelings of trepidation, questions, and uncertainties that we tap into the wellspring of flexibility inside, encouraging a climate of realness and self-empathy.

Flexibility arises as a robust friend on the excursion towards supporting internal strength. It isn't the shortfall of provokes yet the capacity to return from mishaps that characterizes strength. The supporting murmurs advise us that misfortunes are not inseparable from disappointment however are potential open doors for development and self-acknowledgment. The idea of versatility stretches out past individual encounters to envelop the aggregate strength of networks that rise like a phoenix after despair, exhibiting the unyielding human soul.

The supporting murmurs of internal strength interlace with the subject of human association. Connections structure the multifaceted strings that weave the texture of our reality, and it is in the bonds we manufacture with others that the supporting murmurs track down reverberation. Whether through shared looks, soothing contacts, or basic uplifting statements, human association turns into a wellspring of solidarity and versatility. The supporting murmurs highlight the aggregate energy that ties hearts and spirits together, accentuating the meaning of local area and shared encounters in the embroidered artwork of life.

Chasing after supporting internal strength, the idea of validness becomes the overwhelming focus. Society frequently forces tight meanings of solidarity, stressing unemotional disposition, resolute purpose, and an enduring outside. Be that as it may, the supporting murmurs challenge these inflexible develops, welcoming us to embrace realness as an extreme demonstration of rebellion. Genuine strength, the murmurs remind us, lies not in that frame of mind of weakness but rather in the fortitude to be blemished, powerless, and valid.

A positive mentality arises as a critical part in the development of internal strength. The supporting murmurs guide us in keeping an eye on the nursery of our viewpoints, getting rid of cynicism, and sustaining the seeds of positive thinking. Inspiration isn't a forswearing of reality yet a cognizant decision to zero in on potential outcomes and open doors in the midst of life's difficulties. It is from the perspective of a positive outlook that we hear the supporting murmurs most obviously, mixing each part of our lives with expectation and reason.

Taking care of oneself turns into an essential support point in the excursion towards supporting internal strength. The murmurs advocate for a comprehensive way to deal with prosperity, underscoring the supporting of the body, psyche, and soul. A long way from being an extravagance, taking care of oneself is a promise to sustaining oneself truly, inwardly, and profoundly. It is through taking care of oneself that we develop the versatility expected to explore the back and forth movement of life, cultivating a feeling of equilibrium and prosperity.

The supporting murmurs welcome us to develop a feeling of appreciation as we cross the scenes of our lives. Appreciation turns into a string that ties the texture of our reality, winding through snapshots of satisfaction, examples learned, and the versatility acquired.

Offering thanks, both for the conventional and remarkable, turns into a training that improves our consciousness of the supporting murmurs and cultivates a profound appreciation for the wealth of life.

Care arises as an integral asset chasing supporting internal strength. In a world that frequently pulls us in different headings, care turns into a compass that guides us back to the current second. It is in the tranquility of care that we hear the supporting murmurs most plainly, for it is right now that the pith of internal strength is felt. Care is certainly not a transient practice yet an approach to being - a cognizant mindfulness that imbues each breath and each step with aim and reason.

The supporting murmurs of inward strength track down articulation in the subject of versatility. Flexibility is definitely not a quality held for a limited handful yet a limit that lives inside every person. It is the capacity to adjust, return, and flourish despite misfortune. The supporting murmurs guide us in saddling the force of flexibility, for it is through versatility that we change difficulties into impetuses for development.

The idea of weakness stays at the very front of the excursion towards supporting inward strength. It is in recognizing our weaknesses that we tap into the wellspring of solidarity inside. Weakness isn't a shortcoming however an entryway to validness and association. The supporting murmurs welcome us to embrace our weaknesses, for it is in the hug that we find the strength that lies underneath the surface.

Giving up turns into a subject woven into the story of supporting internal strength. It's anything but an acquiescence yet a delivery - an arrival of connections, assumptions, and the requirement for control. Giving up liberates us from the weights that burden us, permitting the supporting murmurs to direct us towards a lighter, more freed presence. It is through the craft of giving up that we make space for development, restoration, and the spreading out of our inward strength.

The supporting murmurs entice us to develop a feeling of interest and transparency. Life is an unending excursion of revelation, and it is in the receptiveness to new encounters, viewpoints, and conceivable outcomes that we tap into the unfathomable repositories of inward strength. The supporting murmurs are a call to wander past the recognizable, to investigate the unfamiliar domains of our true capacity, and to embrace the developing idea of our own reality.

In the midst of the hardships of life, the supporting murmurs of internal strength track down comfort in the force of association. Human association, whether through connections, local area, or shared encounters, is a wellspring of solidarity and flexibility. It is in the aggregate embroidery of mankind that the supporting murmurs become a chorale, resounding with the common battles and wins of people and networks.

As we consider the supporting murmurs of internal strength, we are helped to remember the exchange among light and shadow, happiness and distress, achievement and disappointment. The supporting murmurs guide us in embracing the full range of human experience, advising us that strength isn't the shortfall of weakness yet the fortitude to defy and rise above it. In the amazing orchestra of life, the supporting murmurs fit with the subject of mindfulness, stressing the significance of noticing ourselves without judgment and scattering the shadows of self-uncertainty and dread.

The idea of pardoning becomes basic to the excursion towards supporting inward strength. Pardoning, both towards oneself as well as other people, isn't a supporting of activities however a delivery - an arrival of the shackles that tight spot the soul. It is through the demonstration of pardoning that we free ourselves from the weights of hatred and harshness, permitting the supporting murmurs to direct us towards a way of mending and recharging.

All through our investigation, the supporting murmurs have highlighted the meaning of the excursion, in addition to the objective. It is currently becoming, advancing, and developing that the embodiment of inward strength is generally substantial. The supporting murmurs welcome us to enjoy the experiences, gain from the encounters, and appreciate the development that unfurls with each step.

In the amazing account of supporting inward strength, the job of misfortune can't be disregarded. Misfortune, with its hardships, turns into the cauldron wherein internal strength is manufactured. The supporting murmurs advise us that misfortune isn't an enemy yet an imposing partner that shapes and forms the forms of our personality. It is in confronting difficulty with mental fortitude and versatility that we uncover the genuine profundity of our internal strength.

Trusting in oneself arises as a focal topic in the supporting murmurs of inward strength. It's anything but a presumptuous declaration however a basic affirmation of one's worth and potential. The supporting murmurs guide us in developing a positive mental self portrait, underscoring the significance of the confidence in our capacities and value as a passage to opening the supplies of internal strength.

As we cross the scenes of our lives, the supporting murmurs of internal strength interweave with the topic of compassion. Compassion, the capacity to comprehend and discuss the thoughts of others, turns into an extension that interfaces essences. It is in broadening compassion towards oneself as well as other people that the supporting murmurs become an aggregate chorale, resounding with the common mankind that ties every one of us.

9.2 Tips for maintaining and sustaining inner strength over time

Keeping up with and supporting inward strength over the long run is a nuanced and dynamic cycle that requires a smart and all encompassing methodology. The supporting murmurs of internal strength, as we have investigated all through our excursion, highlight the significance of progressing taking care of oneself, versatility, and an outlook that embraces development and legitimacy. In this part, we will dig into commonsense tips that can act as an aide for developing and supporting inward strength throughout one's life.

A fundamental part of keeping up with internal strength is the act of mindfulness. Normal self-reflection and contemplation make a space for grasping one's considerations, feelings, and responses. Fostering a propensity for care, where one is completely present in the ongoing second without judgment, considers a more profound association with the supporting murmurs of inward strength. This mindfulness frames the bedrock whereupon different tips and practices can be assembled.

1. **Develop a Positive Mentality:**
   A positive mentality is a strong partner in supporting inward strength. It includes deliberately deciding to zero in on the positive parts of life, even notwithstanding difficulties. The supporting murmurs guide us to sustain a hopeful standpoint, perceiving that difficulties are amazing open doors for development. This attitude shift empowers people to explore troubles with strength and see mishaps as transitory as opposed to inconceivable.

2. **Embrace Change and Flexibility:**
   Life is innately unique, loaded up with changes and vulnerabilities. The supporting murmurs energize a mentality that embraces change as a characteristic piece of the human experience. Creating flexibility permits people to explore life's exciting bends in the road with effortlessness and versatility. Embracing change as a chance for learning and development cultivates a feeling of internal strength that can endure the rhythmic movements of life.

3. **Focus on Taking care of oneself:**
   Taking care of oneself is a principal point of support in the excursion of supporting inward strength. It includes making purposeful moves to support one's physical, close to home, and mental prosperity. Normal activity, adequate rest, solid sustenance, and exercises that give pleasure add to a versatile and grounded establishment. The supporting murmurs advise us that taking care of oneself isn't an extravagance however a need for developing the energy and strength expected to confront life's difficulties.

4. **Fabricate and Keep up with Strong Connections:**
   Human association is a strong wellspring of solidarity. The supporting murmurs accentuate the significance of building and keeping up with strong connections. Developing associations with family, companions, and a local area gives an organization of consistent encouragement. These connections offer a space for sharing encounters, looking for direction, and getting consolation, supporting the supporting murmurs of inward strength through shared mankind.

5. **Practice Appreciation:**
   Developing an act of appreciation is an extraordinary apparatus in supporting inward strength. The supporting murmurs guide people to see the value in the positive parts of life, even amidst hardships. Routinely recognizing and offering thanks for little snapshots of euphoria, examples learned, and the help of others cultivates an inspirational outlook. Appreciation turns into a string woven into the texture of day to day existence, improving one's familiarity with the supporting murmurs.

6. **Put down Stopping points:**
   Defining and keeping up with sound limits is essential for protecting internal

strength. The supporting murmurs urge people to perceive their cutoff points and convey them actually. This includes saying no while important, focusing on taking care of oneself, and laying out clear limits in connections and work. Regarding individual limits is a proactive move toward supporting internal strength by forestalling burnout and keeping a feeling of equilibrium.

7. **Participate in Deep rooted Learning:**
The supporting murmurs advocate for a feeling of interest and receptiveness to new encounters. Participating in long lasting realizing, whether through proper schooling, studios, or independent investigation, animates scholarly development and versatility. Nonstop learning cultivates flexibility and a mentality that perspectives challenges as any open doors for gaining new abilities and information.

8. **Cultivate a Feeling of Direction:**
Finding and supporting a feeling of direction is a strong inspiration in supporting inward strength. The supporting murmurs guide people to adjust their activities to their qualities and interests. Developing a reason driven life gives a more profound significance that rises above individual difficulties. It turns into a directing power that injects day to day activities with goal, adding to a strong and deliberate presence.

9. **Practice Care and Reflection:**
The supporting murmurs resound with the act of care and contemplation as devices for keeping up with inward strength. These practices include developing an increased consciousness of the current second, cultivating a feeling of quiet and centeredness. Ordinary care and reflection meetings furnish a space to interface with the supporting murmurs, advancing close to home flexibility and mental clearness.

10. **Develop Adaptability in Objective Setting:**
While laying out objectives is fundamental for self-improvement, the supporting murmurs help us to remember the significance of adaptability in objective setting. Life is dynamic, and conditions might change. Adjusting objectives to line up with developing needs and real factors permits people to explore moves without an unbending connection to explicit results. This adaptability adds to a strong and versatile mentality.

11. **Look for Proficient Help:**
Perceiving the requirement for proficient help is an indication of internal strength. The supporting murmurs urge people to look for the direction of psychological wellness experts, guides, or mentors while confronting difficulties that might feel overpowering. Proficient help gives instruments and procedures to adapting to challenges, building up the supporting murmurs of internal strength through a cooperative and steady methodology.

12. **Participate in Thoughtful gestures:**
The supporting murmurs reverberate with the extraordinary force of gracious-

ness. Taking part in thoughtful gestures, whether little or critical, makes a positive expanding influence. Graciousness towards oneself as well as other people encourages a feeling of interconnectedness and adds to a good and caring outlook. Thoughtful gestures become an impression of the supporting murmurs in real life, building up the obligations of shared mankind.

13. **Observe Accomplishments, Of all shapes and sizes:**
Recognizing and commending accomplishments, paying little mind to estimate, is a training that intensifies the supporting murmurs of internal strength. Finding opportunity to perceive individual achievements, progress, and victories adds to a positive mental self portrait. Festivity turns into a custom that builds up a feeling of achievement and flexibility, energizing the continuous excursion of supporting inward strength.

14. **Take part in Customary Reflection and Journaling:**
The supporting murmurs guide people to take part in customary reflection and journaling for the purpose of self-disclosure and development. Recording contemplations, sentiments, and encounters gives a substantial record of one's excursion. Through reflection, people can acquire experiences into examples, difficulties, and individual qualities, lining up with the supporting murmurs in cultivating continuous mindfulness.

15. **Acknowledge Flaw and Practice Self-Sympathy:**

The supporting murmurs underline the significance of tolerating defect as an inborn piece of the human experience. Rehearsing self-sympathy includes treating oneself with benevolence and figuring out, particularly in snapshots of trouble. Embracing defects and developing self-sympathy add to a strong and genuine feeling of internal strength.

Generally, keeping up with and supporting internal strength is a persistent and purposeful interaction that includes meshing together these different tips and practices into the texture of day to day existence. The supporting murmurs guide people towards a comprehensive methodology that envelops actual prosperity, profound flexibility, positive outlook, and significant associations. By coordinating these tips into one's life, people can develop a vigorous and persevering through internal strength that fills in as an unflinching friend on the excursion of life.

9.3 Encouragement for readers to continue their journey of self-discovery and strength-building

As we finish up this investigation of supporting inward strength through the murmurs that reverberate inside the human spirit, it is critical to offer inspirational statements to perusers who might be on their own excursion of self-disclosure and strength-building. The way towards internal strength is a dynamic and individual one, loaded up with exciting bends in the road, triumphs and misfortunes. The supporting murmurs, as a directing power, ask you to proceed with this excursion with fortitude, strength, and an open heart.

Embrace the Uniqueness of Your Excursion:

Every individual's process is intrinsically remarkable, molded by private encounters, difficulties, and wins. The supporting murmurs advise you that there is nobody size-fits-all way to deal with developing internal strength. Embrace the uniqueness of your excursion, perceiving that your way might veer from others, and that is entirely legitimate. Your encounters, both blissful and testing, add to the extravagance of your internal scene.

Observe Your Advancement, Of all shapes and sizes:

Chasing inward strength, it's critical to recognize and commend your advancement. The supporting murmurs urge you to celebrate both huge achievements and little triumphs. Pause for a minute to consider the means you've taken, the difficulties you've survived, and the development you've encountered. Praising your advancement isn't a demonstration of narcissism yet an acknowledgment of your strength and assurance.

Be Thoughtful to Yourself in Snapshots of Battle:

The supporting murmurs accentuate the significance of self-empathy during snapshots of battle. Confronting difficulties and misfortunes on the excursion towards inward strength is regular. At these times, be caring to yourself. Perceive that defect is important for the human experience, and the murmurs ask you to move toward yourself with a similar sympathy you would offer a companion confronting troubles. Self-consideration is an amazing asset for strength and self-revelation.

Trust the Course of Self-Disclosure:

The excursion of self-disclosure is definitely not a direct way however a ceaseless course of unfurling layers inside yourself. The supporting murmurs urge you to trust this cycle. As you explore the profundities of your own cognizance, show restraint toward yourself. Embrace the vulnerabilities, gain from the difficulties, and trust that each step, regardless of how little, adds to the more extensive material of your self-disclosure.

Track down Strength in Weakness:

Weakness is definitely not an indication of shortcoming, however a passage to realness and association. The supporting murmurs help you that minutes to remember weakness hold significant strength.

At the point when you permit yourself to be open and credible, you make space for development and certified associations. Embrace weakness as a wellspring of versatility, and perceive that genuine strength frequently rises up out of the boldness to be really and proudly yourself.

Construct a Steady Organization:

On this excursion, the supporting murmurs underline the significance of building and sustaining a steady organization. Encircle yourself with people who elevate, energize, and rouse you. Share your encounters, delights, and difficulties with the people who truly care about your prosperity. The supporting murmurs reverberation in the associations you fashion, advising you that you don't need to explore the excursion alone.

Ceaselessly Develop a Positive Outlook:

A positive mentality is a strong partner chasing inward strength. The supporting murmurs guide you to pick idealism, even despite difficulty deliberately. Shift your concentration towards the conceivable outcomes that difficulties present, and view mishaps as any open doors for development. Developing a positive mentality isn't tied in with denying reality however about moving toward existence with versatility, trust, and a faith in your ability to survive.

Embrace Change as a Necessary Piece of Development:

Life is set apart by change, and the supporting murmurs urge you to embrace it as a fundamental piece of your development. Change offers open doors for learning, variation, and change. Instead of opposing change, move toward it with an open heart and a readiness to investigate new skylines. Embracing change lines up with the murmurs' call for flexibility and versatility.

Practice Appreciation for the Excursion:

Appreciation turns into a strong sidekick on your excursion towards inward strength. The supporting murmurs welcome you to develop appreciation for the snapshots of satisfaction, the illustrations learned, and the strength acquired. Get some margin to offer thanks for the help of others, the open doors for development, and the excellence in both the customary and uncommon parts of your excursion. Appreciation amplifies the murmurs of internal strength in your everyday existence.

Trust in Your Intrinsic Strength:

The supporting murmurs reverberation a principal truth - that you have intrinsic strength inside you. Have faith in this strength. Believe that you have the flexibility and fortitude to confront anything challenges come your direction. The murmurs advise you that strength isn't an outer thing to be procured, yet a power that dwells inside, ready to be recognized and developed.

Participate in Demonstrations of Self-Generosity:

Demonstrations of self-graciousness are vital to supporting inward strength. The supporting murmurs guide you to treat yourself with a similar graciousness and sympathy you reach out to other people.

Take part in exercises that give you pleasure, focus on your prosperity, and be aware of your own necessities. Self-consideration is a supporting power that builds up the supporting murmurs and cultivates a positive and tough mentality.

Proceed with the Excursion with Interest and Transparency:

Move toward your excursion of self-revelation with a feeling of interest and receptiveness. The supporting murmurs resound with the possibility that life is a ceaseless investigation. Be interested about your own true capacity, interests, and the bunch prospects that unfurl before you. Remain open to new encounters, viewpoints, and valuable open doors for development. The excursion is continuous, and each step holds the potential for significant self-disclosure.

Recollect that Internal Strength Develops:
Inward strength is certainly not a decent state however a dynamic and developing power. The supporting murmurs advise you that strength develops, extends, and adjusts over the long haul. Embrace the developing idea of your internal strength, understanding that it changes through the encounters, difficulties, and wins you experience. Praise the advancing strength that goes with you on your steadily unfurling venture.

Recognize the Magnificence All the while:
Chasing internal strength, the supporting murmurs urge you to recognize the excellence in the actual process. Becoming zeroed in on arriving at an objective or accomplishing explicit goals is simple. Nonetheless, the murmurs guide you to see the value in the lavishness of the excursion - the snapshots of self-disclosure, the development in versatility, and the magnificence inborn in the unfurling story of your life.

Trust in Your Strength:
Versatility is a vital part of inward strength, and the supporting murmurs remind you to confide in your flexibility. Consider the difficulties you have confronted and survived. Perceive the strength that dwells inside you, permitting you to return quickly, adjust, and flourish. Confiding in your versatility builds up the supporting murmurs, engaging you to confront whatever what's in store holds with certainty.

Keep Looking for Help When Required:
Looking for help is certainly not an indication of shortcoming yet a demonstration of your obligation to self-revelation and development. The supporting murmurs urge you to connect for help when required. Whether through companions, family, guides, or experts, interfacing with others cultivates a feeling of having a place and builds up the supporting murmurs through shared encounters.

Love the Intricacy of Your Humankind:
The supporting murmurs praise the intricacy of your humankind. Embrace the full range of your feelings, encounters, and the layers that make you particularly you.

The murmurs guide you to love both the light and the shadow, perceiving that genuine inward strength rises out of the acknowledgment and incorporation of your whole self.

Show restraint toward Your Excursion:
Persistence is a righteousness on the way of self-disclosure and strength-building. The supporting murmurs advise you that self-awareness is a steady cycle that unfurls voluntarily. Show restraint toward yourself during snapshots of vulnerability or when progress appears to be slow. Believe that each step, regardless of how little, adds to the general woven artwork of your excursion.

Recognize Your Effect on Others:
Your excursion of self-disclosure and internal strength meaningfully affects everyone around you. The supporting murmurs resound in the associations you structure, moving others to set out on their own excursions. Recognize the positive effect you

have on individuals in your day to day existence, and perceive the potential for aggregate development as you keep on sustaining your inward strength.

Track down Satisfaction right now:

In the midst of the goals for development and self-disclosure, the supporting murmurs guide you to track down happiness right now. Life unfurls in the now, and by appreciating the excellence, effortlessness, and favors of the present, you enhance your experience. The murmurs advise you that satisfaction isn't exclusively tracked down in ongoing accomplishments however is a sidekick open to you in every second.